Quantitative Perspectives on Behavioral Economics and Finance

Series Editor
James Ming Chen
College of Law
Michigan State University
East Lansing, Michigan, USA

More information about this series at
http://www.palgrave.com/series/14524

Scott Gilbert

Multi-Market Antitrust Economics

palgrave
macmillan

Scott Gilbert
Southern Illinois University
Carbondale
Illinois
USA

Quantitative Perspectives on Behavioral Economics and Finance
ISBN 978-3-319-69385-9   ISBN 978-3-319-69386-6   (eBook)
https://doi.org/10.1007/978-3-319-69386-6

Library of Congress Control Number: 2017956573

Cover illustration: Détail de la Tour Eiffel © nemesis2207/Fotolia.co.uk

Printed on acid-free paper

This Palgrave Macmillan imprint is published by Springer Nature
The registered company is Springer International Publishing AG
The registered company address is: Gewerbestrasse 11, 6330 Cham, Switzerland

FOREWORD

Heterodox Antitrust Economics

Heterodox Antitrust Economics
Preface to SCOTT GILBERT, MULTI-MARKET ANTITRUST ECONOMICS
(Palgrave Macmillan 2017)
I am delighted to welcome Scott Gilbert and *Multi-Market Antitrust
Economics* to Palgrave Macmillan's series, *Quantitative Perspectives on
Behavioral Economics and Finance*. Professor Gilbert's volume progres-
sively elaborates antitrust economics from a basic model of monopoly to
multi-market scenarios involving spillovers and mergers, and ultimately to
broader economic domains such as international trade. His concluding
chapter on natural monopoly foreshadows the application of antitrust
economics to related legal domains, such as intellectual property[1] and
industry-specific regulation.[2] The transition from single-firm to multi-
market antitrust economics, combined with the promise of connections to
the broader economy, echoes grander aspirations toward comprehensive,
unitary treatments of antitrust and cognate branches of economics.[3]

Professor Gilbert's crisp tour of antitrust economics reflects the incor-
poration of economic thought into legal doctrine,[4] a celebrated history
traceable at least to the Supreme Court's adoption of the "rule of reason"
in the *Standard Oil* decision of 1911.[5] The Sherman Act of 1890, after all,
had left the federal judiciary with an open-ended mandate to draw upon
the common law and other sources of wisdom.[6]

In fixing the boundaries of antitrust liability, the Supreme Court has
often overturned *per se* rules whose legal premises have come under
theoretical and empirical attack. The ascendancy of case-specific economic

analysis in antitrust is perhaps most vividly portrayed in the rejection of *per se* rules and the application of the rule of reason to all vertical restraints: nonprice restraints,[7] maximum resale price maintenance,[8] and minimum resale price maintenance.[9] Even practices nominally subject to *per se* condemnation reflect judicial ambivalence over the competitive consequences of antitrust. Normative ambiguity thus clouds the doctrinal clarity of concerted refusals to deal,[10] predatory pricing,[11] the sharing of pricing information among horizontal competitors,[12] and tying arrangements.[13]

Doctrinal evolution in antitrust law reflects a burgeoning heterodoxy in economic thought that generalist judges have imported into federal courts. For half a century, economic thought associated with the University of Chicago has exerted enormous influence on antitrust.[14] The impact of the "Chicago School" of antitrust economics was especially profound in the law of mergers[15] and vertical restraints,[16] doctrinal domains where the revival of the rule of reason led to a regime of *de facto* legality.[17]

Since the 1980s, a competing post-Chicago school of antitrust economics has emerged.[18] The Chicago school "pre-dated . . . interest among economists" in "game-theoretic analysis of strategic behavior," such as decisions anticipating "rivals' likely reactions" to firm conduct.[19] A competing school of post-Chicago antitrust thought gave rise to works identifying multi-market threats from tying arrangements[20] and the broadly anticompetitive potential of strategies to raise rivals' costs.[21] Post-Chicago scholarship challenges the preeminence of rationality-based, neoclassical thought in antitrust law and economics.[22] A "Neo-Chicago" school of antitrust thought engages insights associated with post-Chicago analysis in an effort to reassert the primacy of formally rational decisionmaking.[23]

A distinct body of *behavioral* antitrust economics has now entered the fray.[24] J. Thomas Rosch, Federal Trade Commissioner, has explicitly embraced the application of behavioral economics to antitrust enforcement.[25] Because behavioral economics directly challenges the assumption that economic actors are rational,[26] behavioral antitrust has drawn equal measures of ideologically motivated praise and condemnation. While some champions of behavioral antitrust predict that "*Homo economicus* will become extinct" and "the Chicago School's antitrust dominance will come to a timely end,"[27] detractors declare a "behavioral irrelevance theorem" positing that "behavioral economics . . . fails to offer *any* clear policy implications for antitrust."[28]

In a field as dynamic and heterodox as antitrust, categorical pronouncements on economic methodology have no place.[29] Though behavioral economics adopts a psychologically or even biologically informed approach to human and institutional conduct, it does not constitute a methodological, let alone ideological, nullification of the Chicago school's underpinnings in the neoclassical economics of rational expectations. Behavioral finance, for instance, integrates mathematical insights on abnormal markets with psychological evidence of cognitive biases and investor irrationality.[30] Antitrust economics should likewise strive to embrace diversity in methodology—a heterodox commitment that combines intellectual eclecticism, empirical rigor, and explanatory power.

The struggle among competing schools of antitrust thought reflects a parallel tension in finance, a cognate branch of economics that informs legal subjects related to antitrust, particularly the regulation of securities markets and financial institutions. Finance rests upon its own variant of the rational expectations hypothesis[31]—namely, the presence of rational, welfare-maximizing "agents [who] know ...precisely" the "objective probability law describing" the relationship between risk and return and that embodiment of that relationship in asset prices.[32] The expectation that excess return over a risk-free asset "should vary positively and proportionately to market volatility" represents the "first law of finance."[33]

The efficient market hypothesis posits that securities markets incorporate all information into security prices and that the rational pricing of securities prevents "most investors [from] achiev[ing] consistently superior rates of return."[34] The commitment of efficient market hypothesis to rationality plays a role in mathematical finance that is analogous to that of the Chicago school in antitrust.[35] In practice, however, violations of market efficiency abound. The most serious challenges to the efficient market hypothesis include Fama and French's "three-factor" model,[36] the low-volatility anomaly,[37] the equity premium puzzle,[38] and short-term price continuation anomalies such as momentum[39] and post-earnings announcement drift.[40]

The intellectual equivalent of post-Chicago antitrust in mathematical finance addresses "'efficiency-defying anomalies' ... such as market swings in the absence of new information and prolonged deviations from underlying asset values."[41] Critically, though, these anomalies do not have a clear causative etiology. Imperfections in financial information "can lead to the *appearance* of risk premiums or asset pricing anomalies."[42] Investors confronted "with valuation parameter uncertainty" may respond rationally by "pric[ing] stocks in a way that leads to the appearance of deviations from market efficiency."[43] Inconveniently, investor behavior and constrained rationality as competing theories "bear considerable mathematical resemblance to each other" and ultimately "explain similar evidence."[44] It is ultimately "impossible to empirically distinguish between many irrational behavior theories and rational Bayesian models because their predictions are too similar."[45]

As with finance, so with antitrust. In its theoretical and empirical incarnations, antitrust economics should heed the lessons of antitrust doctrine as developed by the Supreme Court. No antitrust claim can survive a motion to dismiss,[46] let alone summary judgment[47] or a motion at trial for a directed verdict,[48] unless it presents facts that are at least as supportive of anticompetitive collusion as they would also support consciously parallel conduct or even wholly independent action.[49]

Although antitrust doctrine does not demand "any particular kind of evidence," it does insist that "the evidence [offered] be of such a quality that it makes collusion" or other anticompetitive behavior "a likely explanation of the activity" at issue.[50] Within such a legal framework, behavioral antitrust should strive to consider "the heterogeneity and variability of market behavior" in order to distinguish how the same "boundedly rational" conduct can generate "rational" but "anticompetitive" business practices alongside "beneficial, procompetitive" arrangements.[51] In situations such as the application of the rule of reason to resale price maintenance,[52] courts taking proper account of behavioral economics should "seek case-specific evidence that sheds light on the nature of" the conduct at issue "and its competitive effects, assigning liability only" when economic conduct, whether formally rational or only boundedly so, "is anticompetitive."[53]

Neoclassical economics, including the Chicago school of antitrust, has come under attack for its failure to reconcile the stylized decisionmaking of *homo economicus* with the actual behavior of *homo sapiens*.[54] For their part, many variants of behavioral economics rely heavily on their own "theories of Everyman ... based mechanically on principles" that presumably bind all of humanity.[55] But even if "Every man is risk averse for gains" in theory, actual experience readily demonstrates that "every man (or woman) is not."[56] Absent more nuanced treatment of actual conduct, purely theoretical behavioral economics offers "a rather blunt tool of analysis," one incapable of "explain[ing] the way all actors make decisions in all contexts."[57]

Competing schools of thought, in antitrust and otherwise, thus fall short of capturing the full complexity of economic conduct:

A starlit or a moonlit dome disdains
All that man is,
All mere complexities,
The fury and the mire of human veins.[58]

In this environment, "antitrust law cannot, and should not, precisely replicate economists' (sometimes conflicting) views."[59] What antitrust economics can accomplish is at once more modest and more helpful. The laudable resort to economic theory in any of its guises, behavioral or otherwise, should never become "detached from economic fundamentals."[60]

This volume on antitrust economics and its broader series on behavioral economics therefore strive to speak of human conduct exactly as it is observed: "[N]othing extenuate/Nor set down in malice."[61] No less in economics than in other manifestations of the human imagination, "the monster and the sleeping queen . . . both have roots struck deep in your own mind."[62] We should therefore treat economics "neither [as] 'a deadly magic and accursed,' [n]or [as] 'blest.'"[63] Instead, it suffices simply to recognize, "It is here."[64]

Michigan State University, College of Law James Ming Chen
East Lansing, MI, USA

NOTES

1. *See, e.g.*, United States v. General Elec. Co., 272 U.S. 476 (1926); FTC v. Actavis inc., 133 S. Ct. 2223 (2013); *cf.* SCM Corp. v. Xerox Corp., 645 F.2d 1195 (2d Cir. 1981) (patent accumulation), *cert. denied*, 455 U.S. 1016 (1982). *See generally* U.S. Department of Justice & Federal Trade Comm'n, *Antitrust Guidelines for the Licensing of Intellectual Property*, 4 Trade Reg. Rep. ¶13,132 (1995); Louis Kaplow, *The Patent-Antitrust Intersection: A Reappraisal*, 97 Harv. L. Rev. 1813–1892 (1984).
2. *See, e.g.*, Credit Suisse Secs. (USA) LLC v. Billing, 551 U.S. 264 (2007); United States v. National Ass'n of Secs. Dealers, 422 U.S. 694 (1975); Gordon v. NYSE, 422 U.S. 659 (1975); Otter Tail Power Co. v. United States, 410 U.S. 365 (1973); Silver v. NYSE, 373 U.S. 341 (1963). Antitrust immunity for participation in legislative, judicial, and/or administrative proceedings raises comparable issues. *See, e.g.*, Eastern R.R. Presidents Conference v. Noerr Motor Freight, Inc., 365 U.S. 127 (1961); United Mine Workers v. Pennington, 381 U.S. 657 (1965); California

Motor Transp. Co. v. Trucking Unlimited, 404 U.S. 508 (1972); Professional Real Estate Investors v. Columbia Pictures Indus., Inc., 508 U.S. 549 (1993); *In re* Union Oil Co., 138 F.T.C. 1 (2004).

3. *Compare* James Ming Chen, Econophysics and Capital Asset Pricing: Splitting the Atom of Systematic Risk 275–284 (2017) (describing the progression from firm-specific effects to comovement with broader market and economy-wide effects as "the baryonic ladder") *with* R.H. Coase, The Firm, The Market, and the Law (1990).

4. *See generally, e.g.*, William E. Kovacic & Carl Shapiro, *Antitrust Policy: A Century of Economic and Legal Thinking*, 14 J. Econ. Persp. 43–60 (2000).

5. *See* Standard Oil Co. v. United States, 221 U.S. 1, 60–66 (1911).

6. *See, e.g.*, State Oil Co. v. Khan, 522 U.S. 3, 20–21 (1997); Business Electronics Corp. v Sharp Electronics Corp., 485 U.S. 717, 732 (1988); National Soc'y of Prof. Eng'rs v. United States, 435 U.S. 679, 788 (1978); Apex Hosiery Co. v. Leader, 310 U.S. 469, 489 (1940).

7. *See* Continental T.V., Inc. v. GTE Sylvania, Inc., 433 U.S. 36, 58–59 (1977) (overruling United States v. Arnold, Schwinn & Co., 388 U.S. 365 (1967)).

8. *See State Oil Co. v. Khan*, 522 U.S. at 22 (overruling Albrecht v. Herald Co., 390 U.S. 145 (1968)).

9. *See* Leegin Creative Leather Prods., Inc. v. PSKS, Inc., 551 U.S. 877, 899 (2007) (overruling Dr. Miles Med. Co. v. John D. Park & Sons Co., 220 U.S. 363 (1911)).

10. *See* Fashion Originators' Guild of Am. v. FTC, 312 U.S. 457 (1941); Klor's, Inc. v. Broadway-Hale Stores, Inc., 359 U.S. 207 (1959); Northwest Wholesale Stationers, Inc. v. Pacific Stationery & Printing Co., 472 U.S. 284 (1985); FTC v. Indian Federation of Dentists, 476 U.S. 447 (1986).

11. *See* Brooke Group Ltd. v. Brown & Williamson Tobacco Corp., 509 U.S. 209, 227 (1993); Weyerhaeuser Co. v. Ross-Simmons Hardwood Lumber Co., 549 U.S. 312 (2007).

12. American Column & Lumber Co. v. United States, 257 U.S. 377 (1921); Maple Flooring Mfrs. Ass'n v. United States, 268 U.S. 563 (1925); United States v. Container Corp., 393 U.S. 333 (1969).

13. *See* Jefferson Parish Hosp. Dist. No. 2 v. Hyde, 466 U.S. 2 (1984); Eastman Kodak Co. v. Image Technical Servs., Inc., 504 U.S. 451 (1992).

14. *See generally, e.g.*, Leah Brannon & Douglas H. Ginsburg, *Antitrust Decisions of the U.S. Supreme Court, 1967 to 2007*, 3:2 Competition Pol'y Int'l 3–23 (Autumn 2007); William H. Page, *The Chicago School and the Evolution of Antitrust: Characterization, Antitrust Injury, and Evidentiary Sufficiency*, 75 Va. L. Rev. 1221–1308 (1989); Richard A. Posner, *The Chicago School of Antitrust Analysis*, 127 U. Pa. L. Rev. 925–948 (1979).

Though opinions vary, the Chicago school is thought to have originated either with Aaron Director & Edward H. Levi, *Law and the Future: Trade Regulation*, 51 Nw. U. L. Rev. 281–296 (1956), or with Robert H. Bork: The Antitrust Paradox: A Policy at War with Itself (1978).

15. *See* United States v. General Dynamics Corp., 415 U.S. 486 (1974).

16. *See* cases cited *supra* notes 7–9.

17. *See generally* Douglas H. Ginsburg, *Vertical Restraints: De Facto Legality Under the Rule of Reason*, 60 Antitrust L.J. 67–81 (1991).

18. *See generally* Jonathan B. Baker, *A Preface to Post-Chicago Antitrust, in* Post-Chicago Developments in Antitrust Law 60–75 (Antonio Cucinotta, Roberto Pardolesi & Roger J. Van den Bergh eds., 2002); Herbert J. Hovenkamp, *Antitrust Policy After Chicago*, 84 Mich. L. Rev. 213–284 (1985); Herbert J. Hovenkamp, *Post-Chicago Antitrust: A Review and Critique*, 2001 Colum. Bus. L. Rev. 258–337.

19. Michael H. Riordan & Steven C. Salop, *Evaluating Vertical Mergers: A Post-Chicago Approach* 63 Antitrust L.J. 513–568, 518 (1995).

20. *See, e.g.*, Dennis W. Carlton & Michael Waldman, *The Strategic Use of Tying to Preserve and Create Market Power in Evolving Industries*, 33 Rand J. Econ. 194–220 (2002); Michael D. Whinston, *Tying, Foreclosure, and Exclusion*, 80 Am. Econ. Rev. 837–859 (1990); *cf.* B. Douglas Bernheim & Michael D. Whinston, *Exclusive Dealing*, 106 J. Pol. Econ. 64–103 (1998).

21. *See generally, e.g.*, Thomas G. Krattenmaker & Steven C. Salop, *Anticompetitive Exclusion: Raising Rivals' Costs to Achieve Power Over Price*, 96 Yale L.J. 209–293 (1986); Janusz A. Ordover, Garth Saloner & Steven C. Salop, *Equilibrium Vertical Foreclosure*, 80 Am. Econ. Rev. 127–142 (1990); Steven C. Salop & David T. Scheffman, *Cost-Raising Strategies*, 36 J. Indus. Econ. 19–34 (1987); Steven C. Salop & David T. Scheffman, *Raising Rivals' Costs*, 73 Am. Econ. Rev. 267–271 (1983).

22. *See generally, e.g.*, Christopher R. Leslie, *Rationality Analysis in Antitrust*, 158 U. Pa. L. Rev. 261–353 (2010).

23. *See generally* How the Chicago School Overshot the Mark: The Effect of Conservative Economic Analysis on U.S. Antitrust Policy (Robert Pitofsky ed., 2008); Daniel A. Crane, *Chicago, Post-Chicago, and Neo-Chicago*, 76 U. Chi. L. Rev. 1911–1933 (2009); David S. Evans & A. Jorge Padilla, *Designing Antitrust Rules for Assessing Unilateral Practices: A Neo-Chicago Approach*, 72 U. Chi. L. Rev. 73–98 (2005).

24. *See generally, e.g.*, James C. Cooper & William E. Kovacic, *Behavioral Economics and Its Meaning for Antitrust Agency Decision Making*, 8 J.L. Econ. & Pol'y 779–800 (2012); Amanda P. Reeves & Maurice E. Stucke, *Behavioral Antitrust*, 86 Ind. L.J. 1527–1586 (2011); Maurice E. Stucke, *Behavioral Economists at the Gate: Antitrust in the Twenty-First Century*,

38 Loy. U. Chi. L.J. 513–591 (2007); Avishalom Tor & William J. Rinner, *Behavioral Antitrust: A New Approach to the Rule of Reason After* Leegin, 2011 U. Ill. L. Rev. 805–864.

25. *See* J. Thomas Rosch, *Behavioral Economics: Observations Regarding Issues That Lie Ahead* (June 9, 2010), available at http://www.ftc.gov/speeches/rosch/100609viennaremarks.pdf; J. Thomas Rosch, *Managing Irrationality: Some Observations on Behavioral Economics and the Creation of the Consumer Financial Protection Agency* (Jan. 6, 2010), available at http://www.ftc.gov/speeches/rosch/100106financial-products.pdf; J. Thomas Rosch, *Antitrust Law Enforcement: What to Do About the Current Economics Cacophony?*, available at http://www.ftc.gov/speeches/rosch/090601bateswhite.pdf.

26. *See, e.g.*, Christine Jolls, Cass R. Sunstein & Richard Thaler, *A Behavioral Approach to Law and Economics*. 50 Stan. L. Rev. 1471–1550 (1998); Russell B. Korobkin & Thomas S. Ulen, *Law and Behavioral Science: Removing the Rationality Assumption from Law and Economics*, 88 Cal. L. Rev. 1051–1144 (2000).

27. Thomas J. Horton, *The Coming Extinction of* Homo Economicus *and the Eclipse of the Chicago School of Antitrust: Applying Evolutionary Biology to Structural and Behavioral Antitrust Analyses*, 42 Loy. U. Chi. L.J. 469–522, 475 (2011).

28. Joshua D. Wright & Judd E. Stone II, *Misbehavioral Economics: The Case Against Behavioral Antitrust*, 33 Cardozo L. Rev. 1517–1553, 1526–1527 (2012); *cf.* Joshua D. Wright, *Abandoning Antitrust's Chicago Obsession: The Case for Evidence-Based Antitrust*, 78 Antitrust L.J. 301–331, 313 (2011) ("[T]he burden of proof for demonstrating [a] greater under-standing" of "*both* firm and consumer behavior . . . remains on behaviorist advocates, and there is little empirical support for that proposition . . . ." (emphasis in original)).

29. *Cf.* FCC v. RCA Communications, Inc., 346 U.S. 86, 97 (1943) ("Merely to assume that competition is bound to be of advantage, in an industry so regulated and so largely closed as is this one, is not enough."); Hawaii Tel. Co. v. FCC, 498 U.S. 771, 776 (D.C. Cir. 1974) (same).

30. *Compare* James Ming Chen, Postmodern Portfolio Theory: Navigating Abnormal Markets and Irrational Investors (2016) *with* James Ming Chen, Finance and the Behavioral Prospect: Risk, Exuberance, and Abnormal Markets (2016).

31. *See generally, e.g.*, Thomas J. Sargent, Rational Expectations and Inflation (1986); John F. Muth, *Rational Expectations and the Theory of Price Movements*, 29 Econometrica 315–335 (1961).

32. Larry G. Epstein & Tan Wang, *Intertemporal Asset Pricing Under Knightian Uncertainty*, 62 Econometrica 283–322, 283 (1994).

33. Evan W. Anderson, Eric Ghysels & Jennifer L. Juergens, *The Impact of Risk and Uncertainty on Expected Returns*, 94 J. Fin. Econ. 233–263, 233 (2009).

34. Richard A. Brealey, Stewart C. Myers & Franklin Allen, Principles of Corporate Finance 330 (10th ed. 2011); *accord* Amgen Inc. v. Connecticut Retirement Plans & Trust Funds 133 S. Ct. 1184, 1192 (2013).

35. *See generally, e.g.*, Eugene F. Fama, *The Behavior of Stock Market Prices*, 38 J. Bus. 34–105 (1965); Eugene F. Fama, *Efficient Capital Markets: A Review of Theory and Empirical Work*, 25 J. Fin. 383–417 (1970); Eugene F. Fama, *Efficient Capital Markets II*, 46 J. Fin. 1475–1617 (1991); Lawrence H. Summers, *Does the Stock Market Rationally Reflect Fundamental Values?*, 41 J. Fin. 591–601 (1986).

36. *See* Eugene F. Fama & Kenneth R. French, *The Cross-Section of Expected Stock Returns*, 47 J. Fin. 426–465 (1992); Eugene F. Fama & Kenneth R. French, *Size and Book-to-Market Factors in Earnings and Returns*, 50 J. Fin. 131–155 (1995); *cf.* Kent D. Daniel & Sheridan Titman, *Evidence on the Characteristics of Cross-Sectional Variation in Stock Returns*, 52 J. Fin. 1–33 (1997).

37. *See, e.g.*, Malcolm Baker, Brendan Bradley & Jeffrey Wurgler, *Benchmarks as Limits to Arbitrage: Understanding the Low-Volatility Anomaly*, 67:1 Fin. Analysts J. 40–54 (Jan./Feb. 2011); Robert A. Haugen & A. James Heins, *Risk and the Rate of Return on Financial Assets: Some Old Wine in New Bottles*, 10 J. Fin. & Quant. Analysis 775–784 (1975); Andrew Ang, Robert J. Hodrick, Yuhang Xing & Xiaoyan Zhang, *The Cross-Section of Volatility and Expected Returns*, 61 J. Fin. 255–299 (2006); *cf.* Edward H. Bowman, *A Risk/Return Paradox for Strategic Management*, 21 Sloan Mgmt. Rev. 17–33 (1980); Edward H. Bowman, *Risk Seeking by Troubled Firms*, 23 Sloan Mgmt. Rev. 33–42 (1982).

38. *See generally* Rajnish Mehra & Edward C. Prescott, *The Equity Premium: A Puzzle*, 15 J. Monetary Econ. 145–161 (1985); Rajnish Mehra & Edward C. Prescott, *The Equity Premium Puzzle in Retrospect, in* Handbook of the Economics of Finance 889–938 (George M. Constantinides, Milton Harris & René M. Stulz eds., 2003).

39. *See generally, e.g.*, Mark M. Carhart, *On Persistence in Mutual Fund Performance*, 562 J. Fin. 457–82 (1997); Louis K.C. Chan, Narasimhan Jegadeesh & Josef Lakonishok, *Momentum Strategies*, 51 J. Fin. 1681–1783 (1996); Tarun Chordia & Lakshmanan Shivakumar, *Earnings and Price Momentum*, 80 J. Fin. Econ. 627–656 (2006); Mark Grinblatt, Sheridan TItman & Russ Wermers, *Momentum Investment Strategies, Portfolio Performance, and Herding: A Study of Mutual Fund Behavior*, 85 Am. Econ. Rev. 1088–1105 (1995).

40. *See generally*, *e.g.*, Jeffrey S. Abarbanell & VIctor L. Bernard, *Tests of Analysts' Overreaction/Underreaction to Earnings Information as an Explanation for Anomalous Stock Price Behavior*, 47 J. Fin. 1181–1207 (1992); Guohua Jiang, Charles M.C. Lee & Yi Zhang, *Information Uncertainty and Expected Returns*, 10 Rev. Accounting Stud. 185–221 (2005).

41. Halliburton Co. v. Erica P. John Fund, Inc., 134 S. Ct. 2398, 2421 (2014) (Thomas, J., concurring in the judgment) (quoting Donald C. Langevoort, *Taming the Animal Spirits of the Stock Markets: A Behavioral Approach to Securities Regulation*, 97 Nw. U. L. Rev. 135–188, 141 (2002)).

42. Jennifer Francis, Ryan Lafond, Per Olsson & Katherine Schipper, *Information Uncertainty and Post-Earnings-Announcement Drift*, 34 J. Bus. Fin. & Accounting 403–433, 404 (2007) (emphasis added).

43. *Id*.

44. Alon Brav & John B. Heaton, *Competing Theories of Financial Anomalies*, 15 Rev. Fin. Stud. 576–606, 589 (2002).

45. Francis, Lafond, Olsson & Schipper, *supra* note 42, at 406.

46. *See* Bell Atlantic Corp. v. Twombly, 550 U.S. 544, 553–554 (2007); Monsanto Co. v. Spray-Rite Serv. Corp., 465 U.S. 752, 764 (1984).

47. *See* Matsushita Elec. Indus. Co. v. Zenith Radio Corp., 475 U.S. 574, 586–87 (1986).

48. *See* Theatre Enterprises, Inc. v. Paramount Film Distrib. Corp., 346 U.S. 537, 541–542 (1954).

49. *See generally*, *e.g.*, Keith N. Hylton, *When Should a Case Be Dismissed? The Economics of Pleading and Summary Judgment Standards*, 16 Sup. Ct. Econ. Rev. 39–66 (2008).

50. Herbert J. Hovenkamp, *The Rationalization of Antitrust*, 116 Harv. L. Rev. 917–944, 925 (2003).

51. Avishalom Tor, *Understanding Behavioral Antitrust*, 92 Tex. L. Rev. 573–667, 663 (2014).

52. *See* Leegin Creative Leather Prods., Inc. v. PSKS, Inc., 551 U.S. 877, 882 (2007).

53. Tor, *supra* note , at 660; *see also* Tor & Rinner, *supra* note 24, at 858–864.

54. *See. e.g.*, Richard H. Thaler, *From Homo Economicus to Homo Sapiens*, 14 J. Econ. Persp. 133–141 (2000).

55. Lola L. Lopes, *Between Hope and Fear: The Psychology of Risk*, 20 Advances Experimental Soc. Psych. 255–295, 283 (1987).

56. *Id*. at 268.

57. Chris Guthrie, *Prospect Theory, Risk Preference, and the Law*, 97 Nw. U. L. Rev. 1115–1163, 1163 (2003).

58. W.B. Yeats, *Byzantium*, *in* Collected Poems 335–336, 335 (Robert Mighall intro. 2016).
59. Leegin Creative Leather Prods., Inc. v. PSKS, Inc., 551 U.S. 877, 914–915 (2007) (Breyer, J., dissenting).
60. Lu Zhang, *The Value Premium*, 60 J. Fin. 67–103, 69 (2005).
61. William Shakespeare, *Othello*, act V, sc. 2, *ll.* 351–352, *in* The Oxford Shakespeare: The Complete Works 819–853, 853 (Stanley Wells & Gary Taylor eds., 1986).
62. Stephen Vincent Benét, John Brown's Body 336 (1990) (1st ed. 1928).
63. *Id.*
64. *Id.*

PROLOGUE

Some years ago I attended a 2-week "boot camp" program—introducing economists to the field of law—sponsored by George Mason University. Inspired by the presentations of law and economics luminaries like George Priest (Yale University) and Robert Cooter (University of California at Berkeley), I was also excited to learn about a growing group of legal scholars with graduate coursework in economics. Since then I have seen one area of law—involving lawsuits against business—from a first-hand perspective, as an economist providing opinions on economic loss. I have also attended antitrust conferences—including the Spring Meeting of the Antitrust Section of the American Bar Association (ABA), and the Hal White Antitrust Conference sponsored by Bates White LLC, and served as volunteer in some ABA Antitrust Law Committee activities.

Economic theory, of the sort I saw applied to law in the George Mason boot camp, is essential for understanding commercial law, but it competes for attention with notions and principles from law and other disciplines. Also, some of the economic theory I've hoped to see discussed in commercial cases has been absent. I realized that I wanted to see more extensively a multi-market or general equilibrium approach to the discussion of commercial law—particularly antitrust law where issues of market power and production efficiency can be insightfully recast from a multi-market or general equilibrium perspective. This longing, for a general equilibrium approach to some essential antitrust economic principles, inspired me to write this book.

This book explores antitrust issues—monopoly, price-fixing, mergers, and so on—from a multi-market or general equilibrium perspective. A monopoly is a situation where there is only one supplier of some good or service to a community. More generally, a supplier of some good or service increases market concentration if its actions limit the ability of some other firms to act as independent suppliers of the same good or service. As a social issue, greater market concentration may lead to problems of equity or fairness in the distribution of income and goods across members of society, and also problems of economic inefficiency—whereby less income or goods are produced than could be produced in a more competitive environment. On the other hand, greater market concentration may have the opposite effect, achieving both equity and efficiency.

Introductory economics textbooks present a model of monopoly that focuses on a single market and the monopolist's anti-competitive effects on that market. This textbook model, the pure monopoly model, cannot describe or predict all the consequences of market concentration. To say more than is possible in the pure monopoly model of some good, additional goods can be introduced. Modern antitrust economics accommodates substitute goods, complement goods, and vertically linked goods. Consumer effects of market concentration depend on the existence of substitutes, complements, and vertical linkage. Research in the field often relies on sophisticated economic models, and there is a big gap between this sort of analysis and what one encounters in introductory texts on antitrust economics. This book attempts to bridge that gap, presenting simple yet formal models of monopoly and mergers that showcase multimarket effects. Readers with an antitrust interest will see nontechnical summaries and conclusions of results in each chapter and section, followed by more formal analysis aimed at the level of an upper-level undergraduate student or a graduate student. End-of-chapter problems underscore and extend key themes and results in the chapters.

The style of this book reflects the author's desire to explore some basic antitrust themes "from scratch," using formal but basic economic models, to achieve something like a select coverage of key themes from introductory textbook antitrust economics—from a perspective that a first year graduate student in economics might find appealing. The reader will find commentary on both classical and modern antitrust economics based on this exploratory exercise. This commentary will hopefully benefit the general economist and lawyer interested in antitrust. Noneconomists may find this book further proof of the economist's inability to reach an unambiguous conclusion: market concentration sometimes hurts consumers, sometimes not. But specific contexts of each outcome are neatly conveyed via economic models, a variety of which appear in this book.

Antitrust economics has logical ties to the economics of industry regulation—via natural monopoly. These ties are essential for understanding some consumer effects of market concentration, and the latter chapters in this book touch on this theme, in the same style as the earlier chapters, as well as a discussion of monopoly, monopsony, and the theory of specialization and exchange. These latter excursions are related in their relative absence of unequal economic power, despite market concentration, in stark contrast to the classical monopoly model in which a single supplier exerts great power, but the typical consumer has negligible power. The economic analysis of market concentration should ultimately include some explicit account of economic power inequality, and hopefully this book hints at allied fields that may provide useful inspiration.[1]

A reader that makes their way through this book will find that the models and analysis is in the style of conventional mainstream "western" or "neoclassical" economics, with profit-maximizing firms and utility-maximizing consumers. All models are static, with no uncertainty or risk. All decisions are short run. Every decision is rational. Even for mainstream economics, this leaves out a good deal, but treatment of dynamics, risk, or bounded rationality would exceed the scope of this brief volume.[2] The Foreword to this book, by James Ming Chen, assays a range of recent research developments, including dynamic models of vertical mergers' effects, and models with limited information or bounded rationality, with the admonition to not confuse any formal economic model with reality.

The neoclassical economic models in this book, based on rational choice by firms and households, are the same sort of models advanced by the "Chicago School"—including Richard Posner and Robert Bork—for the study of market concentration's effects on consumer welfare. The Chicago School has had a big impact on the court's stance toward market concentration—particularly in the area of vertical mergers—contributing to a less aggressive posture toward big business in the last 30 years. But to invoke neoclassical models is not to take a stand with big business: such models offer a simple context in which to reason through possible effects of market concentration, and any shortcomings in the model's assumptions can be addressed in more advanced treatments of the subject. It is perhaps the uncertainty, or doubt, about the evils of antitrust or anti-competitive behavior that presents a problem to courts and government agencies, after reading a tome on modern antitrust economics. Such doubt is counter to nineteenth-century convictions of lawmakers that the days of robber barons must end, convictions which precipitated modern antitrust law. But doubt is healthy and transient in any given antitrust review or lawsuit, as an agency head or judge does eventually decide for or against a potentially anti-competitive business move.[3]

For their support while I wrote this book, I thank my wife Barbara and daughter Sydney. I thank my employer Southern Illinois University Carbondale for the opportunity to carry out the research and writing of this book, Bates and White LCC for sponsoring my attendance at the 2017 Hal White Antitrust Conference, the American Bar Association's Antitrust Committee leadership for providing me opportunities to interact with leading antitrust scholars and practitioners, and James M. Chen, editor of Palgrave Macmillan's Quantitative Perspectives from Behavioral Economics and Finance series, for very helpful comments and suggestions on the book. I also thank Allison Neuburger, assistant editor of Palgrave's Economics and Finance division, for finding opportunities to make this book more than I'd initially imagined and for her tireless work keeping on track.

NOTES

1. In a classic monopoly model, the monopoly firm gets revenue from households, and households get goods from firms. If every household has identical wealth, income, and ownership of the firm, any monopoly "power" of the firm over households is illusory: the households receive all economic profits as owners of the firm. More common is to suppose that the households buying the monopolist's goods have no ownership in the firm—a source of power inequality.

2. While preparing this book I volunteered as part of a group of American Bar Association's Antitrust Committee members, assembling a list of practically relevant recent research papers on antitrust economics. Journals in which such papers appeared, and which may be good places for the frontier-minded reader to explore, include Review of Industrial Organization, Managerial and Decision Economics, Economic Inquiry, American Economic Review, The Review of Economic Studies, Rand Journal of Economics, Econometrica, and The Journal of Law and Economics.

3. In the world of mergers, an antitrust agency head—of the Federal Trade Commission, for example—need not always make their way to a decision, as the would-be merging parties may withdraw their merger proposal. Similarly, in antitrust court cases the plaintiff—often the US Department of Justice—may drop the suit midstream.

CONTENTS

PART I

Classical Antitrust Economics

CHAPTER 1

Antitrust Law

Abstract Modern antitrust law seeks to protect consumers from anti-competitive business practices. Goods markets with lots of competition among sellers tend to have lower prices—good for consumers—but good deals tend to be fewer when there are fewer firms. A concentration of market power, among few firms, is anti-competitive if it raises prices faced by consumers. The courts and government agencies that enforce antitrust law must decide what sorts of business practices are significantly anti-competitive. Economic models and analysis play a key role in such decisions, and this book will discuss a variety of economic models in which antitrust issues can be cast.

Before presenting economic models of antitrust issues, it's helpful to overview antitrust law. The focus of this chapter is on US antitrust statutes and case law, with mention of developments elsewhere. In addition to mentioning key legislation like the Sherman Act and Clayton Act, this chapter considers the development of economic ideas that flanked such legislation, including Alfred Marshall's economic theory of competition and monopoly and the "Chicago School" antitrust theory advanced by Robert Bork, Richard Posner, and others. The development of antitrust law and allied economic theories has benefited from critiques along the way, from economists, judges, and others, and this chapter tries to convey antitrust law and economic theory as works in progress.

© The Author(s) 2018
S. Gilbert, *Multi-Market Antitrust Economics*, Quantitative
Perspectives on Behavioral Economics and Finance,
https://doi.org/10.1007/978-3-319-69386-6_1

Keywords Antitrust • Anti-competitive • Law • Competition • Statute • Monopoly

1.1   ECONOMIC PRINCIPLES OF ANTITRUST LAW

Some economic principles consistent with antitrust law—in the United States and other countries like Canada, the United Kingdom, and the European Union— are as follows[1]:

1. Competitive markets tend to produce good economic outcomes for society.
2. Free trade tends to produce efficient resource allocations and satisfied consumers.
3. Actions by firms that block market access, limit trade, or artificially raise consumer prices, impose a cost on society, leading to inefficient resource allocation and lower consumer welfare.
4. Antitrust law provides useful preventatives, punishments, and remedies for offensive and injurious anti-competitive behavior by firms.

1.2   ANTITRUST THEME: DON'T RIP OFF CONSUMERS

Getting ripped-off feels bad. For example, in grade school I saved up some money and bought a box of candies—called "Everlasting GobStoppers"—and brought it to school to set up shop and sell to my classmates after class. As I set up shop, a crowd of classmates gathered and as I named my price and tried to make my first sale, furtive hands snatched candies from the box. Before I knew it, I'd lost most of my inventory and ended up losing most of my savings. I'd planned to make a profit by charging my classmates more per candy than they'd likely pay at the "five-and-dime" store I bought candy from. Was I planning to rip them off? Or make a fair and reasonable profit? At age 11, and lacking an economics education at the time, I could not have answered those questions. I was sure then, as I am now, that my classmates ripped me off, pure and simple.

The term "rip-off" conveys violence—a violent separation of cash from wallet, purse, or bank account. Getting ripped-off is not fair, at least not to the victim, and probably not to society at large. The United States, which inherits much of its legal traditions and procedures from medieval England, has written laws—or *statutes*—and judges' written decisions and opinions, or *case law*, that spell out what it means in the United States to rip someone off badly enough to run afoul of the law. Corresponding laws in other British ex-colonies, specifically Canada and Australia, and European Union countries, are broadly similar.

If a rip-off is an outright theft, or more subtly a fraud, then it is a crime and in the domain of criminal law. If neither theft nor fraud, a rip-off may not be a crime yet be offensive enough to warrant some legal remedy or corrective action in *civil* law. For example, in college I traveled with a friend to a Zen Buddhist retreat in Canada, and while driving back we filled up at a Canadian gas station that accepted our US dollars but as one-for-one with Canadian dollars, whereas US dollars were worth more than Canadian dollars in the open market. Like many rip-off victims we didn't notice what happened until later. The transaction itself could have been a fraud, but given the somewhat hazy circumstances was more likely a matter of civil law—for Canadian courts.

US antitrust law exists to provide legal remedies and corrections to price gouging by businesses, and similar sorts of rip-offs that the public is prone to. The founders of modern legal institutions (judges and the legislature) have generally aimed at expressing legal ideas in easy-to-understand terms, the term "antitrust" is potentially confusing: "trust" sounds like a good thing, and "antitrust" a bad thing, but the aim of antitrust law is not to force a bad outcome on the public. Instead, "trust" represents a situation where businesses in a given industry make a pact to set a high price for the sale of goods to the public, possibly setting up a special committee or "trust" to do the dirty work. Private meeting rooms, shades drawn, many in the back of restaurants and bars, have hosted many such "trust" meetings. By the turn of the twentieth century, such trusts had become so common and notorious in the United States that the government wrote laws that established remedies and penalties for "trust" sorts of collusion price-fixing and other sorts of offensive anti-competitive behavior. Antitrust law aims at trust-busting, or destroying the anti-competitive pacts that would otherwise allow businesses to rob consumers blind.

US antitrust laws, or statutes, most famously consist of the Sherman Antitrust Act of 1890 and the Clayton Antitrust Act of 1914, the former criminalizing the restraint of trade or commerce via "contract, combination in the form of trust or otherwise, or conspiracy," the latter a follow-up that expands the list of offensive anti-competitive behavior to include *price discrimination*—charging one customer more than another for noneconomic reasons, and *tying* or *bundling*—forcing buyers of one good to buy a related good. The Clayton Act does not call offenders of the latter sort criminals but allows people, businesses, and the government (via the Federal Trade Commission[2] and other agencies)—to sue offenders in federal court. [...treble damages ...] Taken together, the Sherman and Clayton Acts place into US criminal and civil law punishments and remedies for common sorts of offensive anti-competitive behavior, or rip-offs, by firms.

By the 1930s the US government determined that ripping off household consumers was not the only sort of anti-competitive behavior worthy of legal remedy and correction. The Robinson-Patman Price Discrimination Act of 1936 added to list of anti-competitive offenses forms of price or deal discrimination whose immediate harm was to other businesses rather than household customers. The Act made it illegal for a business to lower its price below a long-run business-sustainable level to force its weaker competitors to match the low price and thereby go bankrupt. It also made illegal wholesaler price discrimination that involved offering low prices to some retail-level purchases—particularly large chain stores—while offering higher price to other retailers, unless the price differences could be justified in terms of cost of sale. The Act also added more teeth to antitrust law by criminalizing the added offenses.

A roundabout way to rip customers off is to get rid of competing firms and then raise consumer prices. Businesses can do this by consolidating—with smaller firms merging into bigger ones, or one firm being acquired by another. Antitrust law provides checks on these activities, as in the Clayton Act (1914), Celler-Kefauver Act (1950), and the Hart-Scott-Rodino Antitrust Improvements Act (1976) which requires sufficiently large businesses to notify the Federal Trade Commission of their intent to carry out a merger or acquisition and to receive FTC approval.

The reader can find statements of the Sherman Act, Clayton Act, and so on, online, or can "go for broke" and find a complete statement—about 47 pages currently—of US federal statues on monopoly and other offensive or injurious anti-competitive behavior, in Chap. 1 of Title 15 of the US Code, which I will call the Antitrust Code and which is currently available online from US Congress at uscode.house.gov.

Antitrust law is also called competition law as its aims to protect competition. Many countries have antitrust or competition laws similar to that of the United States. In Canada, the Competition Act of 1889 predates the US Sherman Act (1890) by one year and is the world's first competition and antitrust statute. The United Kingdom, Australia, and the European Union countries have antitrust/competition statutes similar to that of the United States and Canada.

The US Antitrust Code contains economic terms and phrases like monopoly, concentration of economic power, free competition, trade, commerce, contract, market price, profit, production, consumer goods, and distribution of goods and services. On the other hand, the Code generally lacks detailed economic discussion and excludes relevant terms familiar to today's economist, including competitive equilibrium, marginal revenue, marginal cost, producer surplus, consumer surplus, deadweight loss, consumer utility function, wage, household budget constraint, production function, economic efficiency, and oligopoly.

While the Antitrust Code contains only limited discussion of economic principles related to anti-competitive behavior, there is plenty of discussion elsewhere on how the Code may be interpreted in economic terms. Some of this discussion appears in studies of the Code commissioned by the government, and a great deal more appears in judges' written opinions on antitrust cases they have reviewed or presided over. The next two subsections briefly summarize the commissioned studies, or critiques, and antitrust legal decisions or case law.

1.3   STUDIES OF ANTITRUST STATUTES

The term "antitrust statue" may sound dull or foreboding, like an ancient and dusty statue of some stern Roman senator, and studies of such may sound worse. But well-written studies can liven a topic up and make it easier to understand. They can also help to improve antitrust law.

As noted in the Antitrust Code, the US government has commissioned three studies on the Code itself, resulting in three reports, one produced long ago in year 1941, one much later in 1979, and one recently in 2007. As a sort of report card, each report generally supported the Code in existence at the time the report appeared but offered some specific recommendations for improvement. The reports are each much longer than the current Code itself, with extensive economic discussion summarized in the paragraphs below.

The 1941 report[3] backed the then-current Antitrust Code in its support of the "competitive system of private capitalism" and its potential to counter the "uneconomic concentration of economic power." The report also recommended a more stringent and proactive merger/acquisition vetting procedure, some stiffer antitrust penalties, and limits on "patent monopoly"—with universal licensing of patents at reasonable fees.[4]

The 1979 report[5] suggested a need for streamlining antitrust cases, which often took months or years to try in court, but also for greater consistency and clarity in the statement of relevant economic issues, including markets:

> Monopoly power presumes a well-defined market within which the defendant can raise price without a significant shift to substitutes. By dealing directly with monopoly power, sound market definition will be encouraged and should result.

The report also called for better economic analysis:

> Where conduct directly evidences existing power, it should be admitted. However, tailoring conduct evidence to proof of current market power, and eliminating the existing incentives to prove a monopoly firm "good" or "bad" in itself, should streamline both the discovery process and the trial and should sharpen the analytical framework for proof of the case.

and included economic terms and phrases absent from the Antitrust Code, including market entry, economic efficiency, deadweight loss, income redistribution, consumer welfare, consumers' willingness to pay, economic analysis, and economic research.

The 2007 report[6] broadly found the Antitrust Code to be in good shape but suggested some changes, including the repeal of Robinson-Patman Act—on the grounds that it protects competitors not competition, improvement of the merger review process—with more consideration of possible efficiencies resulting from mergers and improvement in the quality of the US patent application and review process.

In addition to officially mandated studies of antitrust statutes, there are many published books and articles on antitrust by legal scholars and economists, including Aaron Director, Robert Bork, and Richard Posner—three leading figures in the "Chicago School" of antitrust economic thought. In response to the 2007 report by the

Antitrust Modernization Commission, Robert Bork wrote a letter to the Commission stating: "The antitrust laws, in my opinion, are performing well, in fact better than at any time in the past seventy-five years. It follows that I think there is very little need for 'modernization.'" He goes on to encourage the repeal of the Robinson-Patman Act and to limit what he viewed as too many unmerited private antitrust lawsuits with no legitimate claims of loss to consumer welfare.[7]

1.4 ANTITRUST COURT CASES

The courts have the sometimes-hard job of applying government statutes, and for those court decisions that get appealed, some eventually make it to the highest court—which in the United States is the Supreme Court. Supreme Court decisions are the final say, and so carry greatest "precedential" value among all court decisions, providing precedent and guidance for the court in trying future cases. The collection of Supreme Court decisions on antitrust cases, as well as decisions of lower appellate federal courts, comprises the bulk of US antitrust "case law." The court decisions most highly cited in later cases are often ones to be considered most "significant" or "important."

There are many of important antitrust court decisions, addressing specific topics like price-fixing, monopoly, mergers, predatory pricing, bundling and tying, oligopoly, and price discrimination. A comprehensive survey of such decisions would require more pages than this book contains, and the reader can find recent excellent surveys in Elhauge (2008) and Blair and Kaserman (2009).

Of some interest are the first Supreme Court decisions to rely on particular parts of the Antitrust Code. In these decisions the court often tries to interpret the meaning of the Code itself, a job made tough by often terse Code and a lack of prior decisions on how to interpret it.

The first Supreme Court decision to interpret the Sherman Act—the first part of the Antitrust Code to become law—was the case *United States v. E. C. Knight Company*[8] in 1895, sometimes called the "Sugar Trust case." In this case, a number of sugar refining companies merged (via stock sale) together became a monopolist in the sugar refining industry by year 1892, providing most of the sugar that consumers ultimately bought. However, despite their status as a monopoly, there appeared to be some economic efficiencies associated with the merger, and there was little evidence of offensive anti-competitive behavior: the firm did not slash the amount of sugar sold—instead the amount rose after the merger—and the firm did not raise sugar price much, if at all. The Supreme Court concluded that, while the defendant(s) in the case did act as a monopolist in sugar refining, it did not restrain trade or violate the Sherman Act.

The Court's conclusion in the Sugar Trust case became a precedent for later courts: the existence of a monopoly in an industry does not imply that the monopolist's behavior—per force anti-competitive—is offensive or injurious. Shortly thereafter, William Howard Taft coined the term "rule of reason" to capture the idea that courts should not immediately identify anti-competitive harm with market concentration, in a Sixth Circuit Court of Appeals decision on the case *Addyston Pipe and Steel Co. v. United States* which was affirmed by the Supreme Court in 1899 and became a major precedent for future courts' interpretation of the Sherman Act.[9] Price-fixing, on the other hand, is obviously anti-competitive and "per se" illegal from the courts' standpoint; see *United States v. Trenton Potteries*—273 U.S. 392, year 1927.

The first Supreme Court decision to interpret the Clayton Act was *United States v. United Shoe Machinery Co.* in year 1918,[10] in which the defendant bought some patents on shoe machinery inventions and leased machinery—using the inventions—to shoe manufacturers. The government argued that, while the evidence was mixed, it did not run afoul of the Clayton Act—in which such leases would be unlawful if there effect "may be to substantially lessen competition or tend to create monopoly in any line of commerce." With "may" being a crucial modifier in the last phrase, the Court did not find convincing evidence that the defendant actually did or necessarily would lessen competition or create monopoly, at least not in an obnoxious or injurious way. The result is similar to the Court's decision in *United States v. E. C. Knight Company*, and again required the court to interpret a new law.

For merger law, an important case involving the Clayton Act—as amended in 1950—is *Brown Shoe Company Inc. v. United States* 370 U.S. 294 (year 1962). In its 1962 ruling on this case, the Supreme Court found the 1956 merger of Brown Shoe Company Co. and G. R. Kinney Co. to be illegal and also provided a detailed account of considerations—aside from market concentration—that may be important in evaluating anti-competitive harm from mergers.[11,12] The Court also emphasized a need to protect competition, but not necessarily to protect competitors, a view that would help shape the modern antitrust landscape.

1.5 PROBLEMS

1. Antitrust law has an economic rationale and is broadly consistent with four principles listed earlier. For each of these principles, listed again below, provide the requested commentary.

   (a) For the following statement, give an example of what "markets" and "economic outcomes" might mean: Competitive markets tend to produce good economic outcomes for society.

   (b) For the following, give an example of what "resource" might mean: Free trade tends to produce efficient resource allocations and satisfied consumers.

   (c) For the following, give an example of what "cost" might mean: Actions by firms that block market access, limit trade, or artificially raise consumer prices, impose a cost on society, leading to inefficient resource allocation and lower consumer welfare.

   (d) For the following, give an example of what "preventatives" and "remedies" might mean: Antitrust law provides useful preventatives, punishments, and remedies for offensive and injurious anti-competitive behavior by firms.

2. Read the Sherman Act of 1890 online. Does the word "competition" appear in the Act, and does it matter? Explain.

3. The Sherman Act imposes criminal penalties for some anti-competitive actions, while the Clayton Act imposes civil (noncriminal) penalties and remedies for other anti-competitive actions. Browse and compare the text of the Sherman Act and Clayton Act. Do the offenses described in the Sherman Act seem more heinous or "criminal" than those named in the Clayton Act? Explain.

4. The United States and Canada both passed antitrust/competition statues in the late 1800s. Before that, these countries relied on *common law*—the set of court decisions on what is legal and how illegal acts should be dealt with—for antitrust/competition issues, in a style inherited from British common law. What advantage might the US and Canadian legislatures have seen in creating antitrust/competition statutes in the late 1890s?

5. Browse the Clayton Act and the Federal Trade Commission (FTC) Act, and explain the mandated role of the Federal Trade Commission (FTC) in enforcing antitrust law in the Clayton Act.

6. The US government ordered three studies of US antitrust law, and these were published in years 1941, 1979, and 2007, as discussed

earlier. Read the first few pages of each report, and note the names of the reports' authors. Check out the authors online. What percent of the authors you can find were/are economists or scholars with some economics background?

7. Some have argued that an economist should serve as a member of the US Supreme Court. Do you think that having an economist on the Supreme Court would lead to changes in antitrust case law? If so, how, and if not, why?

8. Read the US Supreme Court's opinion on the case United States v. E. C. Knight Co. (1895).

   (a) The Court seems to indicate that refined sugar is a "necessary of life." Do you agree?

   (b) How does the Court interpret and apply the Sherman Act in this case?

   (c) Often courts will cite previous cases—or case law—in support of their opinions. Did the Court cite case law here?

   (d) US tariff policy restricts the supply of imported sugar into the United States, in part to protect US sugar producers. Was the court protecting the sugar refining defendants in United States v. E. C. Knight Co.?

NOTES

1. The term "antitrust law" is used mainly in the United States, while "competition law" is commonly used in Canada and Europe.

2. The Federal Trade Commission was established via the Federal Trade Commission Act of 1914.

3. The report is entitled "Investigation of Concentration of Economic Power: Final Report," by the Temporary National Economic Committee, runs about 783 pages and is viewable online in single-page browsing format and document-wide word search at babel.hathitrust.org.

4. Patents are a sanctioned sort of monopoly that rewards innovators with exclusive claim to innovation profits, for a period of time.

5. Entitled "Report to the President and the Attorney General of the National Commission for the Review of Antitrust Laws and Procedures," by the National Commission for the Review of Antitrust Laws and Procedures, runs about 329 pages, and like the 1941 report is online at babel.hathitrust.org. The 1979 report was by Executive Order (President Jimmy Carter), while the 1941 report was a "Congressional Investigation of Monopoly."

6. Entitled "Antitrust Modernization Commission: Report and Recommendations," by the Antitrust Modernization Commission, runs about 540 pages, is available online at, for example, govinfo.library.unt.edu, and was commissioned by Congress.
7. Posner (1975, 1976) and Bork (1977) discuss anti-competitive harms of market concentration in terms of consumer welfare or surplus, though in somewhat different terms. See Chap. 2 of this book for more on consumer surplus.
8. The Court's written decisions are available online at the Court's website supreme.justia.com, by searching for the case title and year. For the search "United States v. E. C. Knight Company (1895)," the decision returned is entitled "United States v. E. C. Knight Co. 156 U.S. 1 (1895)," where "156 U.S. 1" refers to volume 156, page 1, of the printed US Reports— which publishes all US Supreme Court decisions and which is the only official version of them.
9. The rule of reason played a significant role in the Supreme Court's subsequent ruling (1911) case *Standard Oil Company of New Jersey v. United States*. See also *Chicago Board of Trade v. United States*—246 (U.S. 231, year 1918).
10. Full citation: United States v. United Shoe Machinery Co. 247 U.S. 32, year 1918.
11. Chief Justice Earl Warren, in delivering the opinion of the Court, wrote: "Statistics reflecting the shares of the market controlled by the industry leaders and the parties to the merger are, of course, the primary index of market power; but only a further examination of the particular market—its structure, history and probable future—can provide the appropriate setting for judging the probable anti-competitive effect of the merger."
12. For recent discussion see Skitol and Vorasi (2012).

REFERENCES

Blair, R. D., & Kaserman, D. L. (2009). *Antitrust economics* (2nd ed.). New York: Oxford University Press.

Bork, R. H. (1977). *The antitrust paradox, a policy at war with itself.* New York, NY: Basic Books.

Elhauge, E. (2008). *United States antitrust law and economics.* New York: Foundation Press.

Posner, R. A. (1975). The social costs of monopoly and regulation. *The Journal of Political Economy, 83*(4), 807–828.

Posner, R. A. (1976). *Antitrust law: An American perspective.* Chicago, IL: The University of Chicago Press.

Skitol, R. A., & Vorasi, K. M. (2012), The remarkable 50-year legacy of *Brown Shoe Co. v. United States. Antitrust, 26*(2), 47–53.

CHAPTER 2

Pure Monopoly Model

Abstract The classical model of the anti-competitive and socially undesirable monopoly is the pure monopoly model. In this model, the monopolist provides less output—at a higher price—than would be provided by competitive firms facing the same production costs. The output drop and price hike are both anti-competitive negative consequences to consumers of monopoly. The model accommodates other measures of anti-competitive harm, including changes in consumer surplus and total surplus.

This chapter discusses the classical model of pure monopoly, under the additional simplifying assumptions that consumer behavior is consistent with a linear demand curve, and firms' technology is consistent with a flat marginal cost curve. There are few parameters in this version of pure monopoly, and this chapter states various anti-competitive monopoly consequences in terms of these parameters. The habit of explicit parameterization carries forward to later chapters in the book, permitting a very basic formal analysis of some antitrust themes.

Under the special assumptions maintained here, a monopoly takeover of a competitive market is bad to a degree that depends on the measure of "badness." Output drops by half, price rises by a factor that depends both on consumers' maximum willingness to pay and on firms' marginal cost, total surplus falls by 25 percent, and consumer surplus falls by 75 percent. The hefty drop in consumer surplus is striking and relevant to modern antitrust analysis that emphasizes consumer surplus effects.

© The Author(s) 2018
S. Gilbert, *Multi-Market Antitrust Economics*, Quantitative
Perspectives on Behavioral Economics and Finance,
https://doi.org/10.1007/978-3-319-69386-6_2

Keywords Pure monopoly • Anti-competitive • Marginal cost • Demand curve • Consumer surplus • Total surplus

2.1   ANTITRUST AND ECONOMIC MODELS

Laws, or statutes, exist that can be put to use by the government or aggrieved parties when confronted with offensive antitrust or anti-competitive behavior. The "how" of putting the statutes to work is where the courts come in, as discussed earlier in the US Supreme Court cases *United States v. E. C. Knight Company* and *United States v. United Shoe Machinery Co.* Recall that Sherman Act, as a written document, is only about two pages long. Applying the Sherman Act in particular cases requires the government—courts and government agencies—to take a close look at markets and the economics going on in markets. Consider, for example, the following key part of the Sherman Act:

> Every person who shall monopolize, or attempt to monopolize, or combine or conspire with any other person or persons, to monopolize any part of the trade or commerce among the several states, or with foreign nations, shall be deemed guilty of a felony. . .

The US federal government, mainly the Department of Justice, has the job of enforcing this part of the Sherman Act, and for this the government needs to know what markets exist for trade "among the several states" and needs to keep tabs on businesses that may try to monopolize trade in some good or service. With many goods and services produced and distributed in and among US states each year, the government has a big job keeping track of them.

The brevity of some antitrust statutes makes possible absurd outcomes. For example, suppose a company L-Scratch, based in Oregon, is the nation's only producer of left-handed back scratchers.[1] If the company starts selling its products in California, has it committed a felony? Hopefully not, but it does monopolize Oregon-California trade in left-handed back scratchers, so why does the Sherman Act not make L-Scratch a criminal enterprise? One reason may be that if no other company has bothered to make left-handed back scratchers, then L-Scratch is automatically a monopoly and does not "monopolize" offensively or obnoxiously. Another may be that, if L-Scratch has a patent on the left-handed back scratcher, then it is legally entitled to monopolize. Here antitrust law may bump up against patent law, awkwardly.

US federal statutes covering antitrust law, specifically Chapter 1 of Title 15 in the US code, currently run about 46 pages, not a long read. The range of possible situations in which a lack or loss of market competition might be harmful is far greater than the range of actual cases considered by Congress when writing the antitrust statutes. The Justice Department and Federal Trade Commission (FTC) have to apply antitrust law but also figure out what it should mean in particular cases.

To successfully apply antitrust law, courts and government agencies need some leeway in interpreting it, as in *United States v. E. C. Knight Company* and *United States v. United Shoe Machinery Co.* They also need access to information or data on markets. In addition to broad market data, they can compel businesses to report prices charged, customer names, and goods quantities produced. Market and company data shed light on the extent of possible monopoly or other sorts of anti-competitive arrangements or behavior.

For example, if in the industry for personal computer operating systems one company—call it M—has a 90 percent market share (selling 90 percent of all pc operating systems that customers buy), then that company is dominant.[2] Whether company M "monopolizes" in some offensive or injurious way is unclear without more data, but what kind of data? Without some economic model of injurious monopoly, the court may not know.

2.2   THE PURE MONOPOLY MODEL

The classic economic model of anti-competitive monopoly effects the pure monopoly model and conforms to the graph in Fig. 2.1.[3] In the graph, market outcomes are shown for some consumer good or service, such as sugar, with the amount sold being a variable attached to the horizontal axis and the sale price being a variable attached to the vertical axis. Implicitly, market outcomes are those that occur during some time period, like year 2016, and in some location, like the United States. For example, in the United States, the price of retail refined sugar in 2016 was about 65 cents, and about 25 million pounds were delivered for domestic food and beverage use.[4]

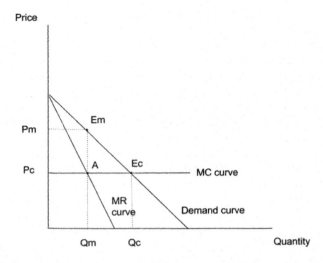

Fig. 2.1 Pure monopoly and economic loss

All else equal, consumers want to purchase greater quantities, and want lower prices. The line labeled "Demand Curve" is the consumers' demand curve, showing the quantity that all consumers would buy of a good— at each given price—assuming that all consumers pay the same price for the good and that each acts as if their quantity choice does not affect price. The line labeled "MR" is the monopolist's marginal revenue—the additional revenue received from each successive unit of good sold— and the horizontal line "MC" is the monopolist's marginal cost, the additional cost incurred from successive units sold, assumed to be the same at each level of output.

The monopolist, as the sole provider of the good, chooses a quantity to supply so as to maximize profit. The monopolist's profit is the difference between its revenue and cost, and maximum profit is reached at that quantity Q_m where marginal revenue equals marginal cost—represented by the crossing point A of the MR and MC curves. The monopolist sells this quantity Q_m at the highest price P_m that consumers are willing to pay. At the monopoly price P_m, the quantity demanded and quantity supplied each equal Q_m, and the economy is in pure monopoly equilibrium. In Fig. 2.1, the monopoly equilibrium point is E_m, which represents the quantity-price pair (Q_m, P_m). There is another point, labeled E_c, which represents the quantity-price pair (Q_c, P_c), with Q_c the competitive equilibrium quantity and P_c the competitive equilibrium price.

In the pure monopoly model, competitive equilibrium is a benchmark point of reference—the economic outcome that would arise if there were many sellers in the market, each having the same marginal cost (MC) and each choosing a quantity for sale so as to maximize their individual profit—while assuming that their quantity choice does not change market price. As shown in Fig. 2.1, competitive equilibrium (E_c) is a market outcome in which consumers get more output and a lower price than they get in monopoly equilibrium (E_m). E_c would be a better deal for consumers than E_m, if they could get it.

Example 2.1 In the US market for cellular phones, let the market demand curve takes the form of the straight line $P = 1000 - 4Q$, with price P on the vertical axis and quantity Q (in millions of phones) on the horizontal axis. The marginal revenue curve is then a straight line $MR = 1000 - 8Q$. Let the marginal cost (MC) of producing a cellular phone be 200 dollars. In competitive equilibrium, MC and demand curves cross: $MC = 200 = 1000 - 4Q$, in which case competitive quantity is $Q_c = 200$ and competitive price is $P_c = 1000 - 4Q_c = 200$. In monopoly equilibrium, MC and MR curves cross: $MC = 200 = 1000 - 8Q$, so the monopolist's quantity is $Q_m = 100$ and their price is $P_m = 1000 - 4Q_m = 600$. In monopoly, consumers pay an extra \$400 per phone, and across all 100 phones sold in monopoly equilibrium, customers pay an overcharge of $400 \times 100 = \$40,000$.

In pure monopoly consumers get a worse deal than with competition, to an extent that is quantified via a higher price paid and lower quantity consumed. To apply the model, the court can try to collect data on the amount of per-unit overcharge (monopoly equilibrium price minus competitive equilibrium price, $P_m - P_c$ in Fig. 2.1) and undersupply (competitive equilibrium quantity minus monopoly equilibrium quantity, $Q_c - Q_m$ in Fig. 2.1). If such data are available, and suggest a significant per-unit overcharge and/or undersupply, the court might view the result as evidence of injurious monopoly.

In the Sugar Trust case *United States v. E. C. Knight Company*, the US Supreme Court had available price and quantity data before and after sugar refining companies banded together to form a monopoly. If the "before" data represent a competitive equilibrium market outcome, and the "after" data correspond to monopoly, then a comparison of "before" and "after" is also a comparison of competition and pure monopoly. As discussed earlier, the Court found that quantity actually rose over time, and price rose but modestly.

The pure monopoly model, with its built-in competitive market benchmark, gives a particular sense in which monopoly can be a bad deal for consumers.[5]

Economic theory provides some additional ways of evaluating the desirability of competitive and monopoly outcomes, in terms of consumer surplus, producer surplus, and total surplus. In Fig. 3.1, *consumer surplus* is the area of the triangle which is above market price (horizontal) line and below the demand curve, *producer surplus* is the area below the market price line and above the marginal cost curve, and *total surplus* is the sum of consumer surplus and producer surplus.

Consumer surplus measures the benefit to consumers of a market outcome, producer surplus measures benefit to producer(s), and total surplus measures benefit to society as a whole. The terminology and graphs associated with these three concepts have changed some since the days of the Sherman Act (1890), but the essential ideas were already in textbook form then—via Alfred Marshall's *Principles of Economics* (1890).[6]

Consumer surplus is higher in competitive equilibrium than in monopoly equilibrium, while producer surplus is higher in monopoly equilibrium. Overall, total surplus is higher in competitive equilibrium, and the drop in total surplus in moving from competitive to monopoly equilibrium is the *deadweight loss* associated with the monopoly—which in Fig. 2.1 is the area of the triangle with corner points E_m, E_c, and A.

Example 2.2 Consider again the cell phone market in Example 2.1. The following table shows values for consumer surplus, producer surplus, and total surplus, for competitive and monopoly equilibrium outcomes.[7]

Equilibrium	Consumer surplus	Producer surplus	Total surplus
Monopoly	2000	4000	6000
Competition	8000	0	8000
Difference	−6000	4000	−2000

As indicated, consumers are better off in competitive equilibrium, with greater consumer surplus there, while the producer is better off in monopoly equilibrium. Society, on the whole, is better of in competitive equilibrium, and the deadweight loss of monopoly equilibrium is the total surplus drop from going from competition to monopoly, here equal to -2000, or just 2000 when measured in absolute terms.

2.3 THE MODEL'S ASSUMPTIONS

The pure monopoly model depicted in Fig. 2.1 includes a linear demand curve and a flat marginal cost curve. Figure 2.1 focuses on these modeling assumptions, labeling the endpoints of the demand curve, and using MC as the numerical value of marginal cost and also the label of the marginal cost curve.

The demand curve shown in Fig. 2.2 has a formula stated again as a numbered equation below—for future reference:

$$\text{Demand:} \quad P = a - bQ \tag{2.1}$$

with a and b positive parameters, and Q in the range $(0, a/b)$.[8] Parameter a represents consumers' maximum willingness to pay for the good, and parameter b represents consumers' required price reduction to purchase one more unit of the good. Both a and b are assumed to be positive. Also, to allow demand and marginal cost curves to cross at some positive quantity Q and price P, it's necessary to suppose that $a > MC$.[9]

The demand curve linearity and flat marginal cost curve flatness assumed here are not necessary to the theory of natural monopoly but are a simple specification often presented in economic texts—see, for example, Mas-Colell et al. (1995, Example 12.B.1) and Nicholson and Snyder (2012, Chapter 18).[10] Also, with the idea of discussing monopoly and related issues in a way that is accessible to both economists and others interested in antitrust, a particularly simple modeling approach makes sense, and the assumptions made here match those in the antitrust works (Posner 1976, Appendix and Blair and Kaserman 2009, Section 3–6).

The crossing point of demand and marginal cost curves is competitive equilibrium, with competitive quantity Q_c and price P_c that have the following formulas[11]:

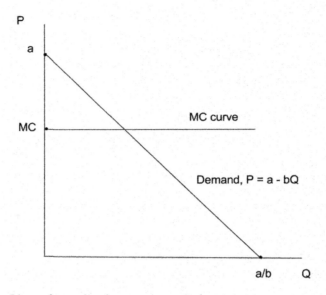

Fig. 2.2   Linear demand and constant marginal cost

$$Q_c = \frac{a - MC}{b} \tag{2.2}$$

$$P_c = MC \tag{2.3}$$

The crossing point of marginal revenue and marginal cost curves yields monopoly equilibrium quantity Q_m, and at that Q_m the corresponding price P_m is determined by the demand curve, in which case[12]:

$$Q_m = \frac{a - MC}{2b}, \tag{2.4}$$

$$P_m = \frac{a + MC}{2}. \tag{2.5}$$

Pure monopoly is anti-competitive, raising price and lowering quantity. Going from competition to monopoly lowers quantity and raises price by amounts we can track using formulas (2.2) through (2.5):

$$Q_c - Q_m = \frac{a - MC}{2b}, \tag{2.6}$$

$$P_m - P_c = \frac{a - MC}{2}, \tag{2.7}$$

each of which is starker when the buyers' maximum willingness to pay a is higher and when marginal cost MC is lower.[13] The overcharge associated with monopoly is $(P_m - P_c)Q_m$. Expressed in terms of demand and cost parameters via formulas (2.2) through (2.5) the overcharge takes the form:

$$\text{overcharge} = \frac{(a - MC)^2}{4b}, \tag{2.8}$$

and is more severe when the gap $a - MC$ between willingness to pay and marginal cost is higher, and when the price drop b, needed to get one more unit of good purchased by consumers, is smaller.

Pure monopoly also has anti-competitive effects on total Marshallian surplus or welfare associated with the marketplace, and Table 2.1 expresses these effects in terms of demand and cost parameters.[14,15,16]

The effect of monopoly is, according to Table 2.1, to cut total surplus by 25 percent relative to the competitive market outcome, regardless of the demand parameters a and b, and production's marginal cost MC. The fact that the 25 percent surplus drop is invariant to parameter values is a result of assuming linear demand and flat marginal cost curves.

A 25 percent reduction in total surplus or welfare may or may not sound like a big anti-competitive problem. On the other hand, from Table 2.1 consumer surplus falls by 75 percent under monopoly, a bigger effect. Changes in surplus, price, and quantity give a range of ways in which to

Table 2.1 Surplus effects of pure monopoly

Equilibrium	Consumer surplus	Producer surplus	Total surplus
Monopoly	$\frac{1}{8}\frac{(a-MC)^2}{b}$	$\frac{1}{4}\frac{(a-MC)^2}{b}$	$\frac{3}{8}\frac{(a-MC)^2}{b}$
Competition	$\frac{1}{2}\frac{(a-MC)^2}{b}$	0	$\frac{1}{2}\frac{(a-MC)^2}{b}$
Difference	$-\frac{3}{8}\frac{(a-MC)^2}{b}$	$\frac{1}{4}\frac{(a-MC)^2}{b}$	$-\frac{1}{8}\frac{(a-MC)^2}{b}$

describe pure monopoly's anti-competitive effects, with no obviously best choice among them. If the goal is to promote consumer welfare, then the monopoly overcharge and drop in consumer surplus are relevant measures of anti-competitive harm.

The change in total surplus triggered by monopoly is the sum of two parts: an increase in producer surplus and a decrease in consumer surplus. Any difference between monopoly's total surplus and consumer surplus effects hinge on the producer surplus or profit effect. Under the maintained assumptions, there is no producer surplus in competitive equilibrium, and from Table 2.1 the increase in producer surplus in monopoly equilibrium is $(2/8)(a - MC)^2/(b)$, while the fall in consumer surplus is $(3/8)((a - MC)^2/(b))$. The change ΔPS in producer surplus is therefore related to the change ΔCS in consumer surplus and to the change ΔTS in total surplus via:

$$\Delta PS = -\frac{2}{3}\Delta CS \tag{2.9}$$

$$\Delta PS = -\frac{1}{2}\Delta TS \tag{2.10}$$

In Posner (1975, 1976), Richard Posner argues that an increase in producer surplus triggered by monopoly should not be counted as an offset to consumer surplus loss, in determining societal harm. From Eqs. (2.9)–(2.10), under the assumptions maintained here, the inclusion or exclusion of producer surplus is a big deal: monopoly profits, that is, the gain in producer surplus, are half the size of the deadweight loss defined by $-\Delta TS$. Deducting producer surplus as a relevant component of total surplus, the remainder is consumer surplus. The idea that consumer surplus is a relevant measure of societal good, when evaluating anti-competitive harm, has gained wide support in antitrust law.[17,18]

The foregoing characterization of pure monopoly effects relies on a linear demand curve and flat marginal cost curve, and results can differ greatly if instead the demand curve is linear or marginal cost curve is increasing. Nicholson and Snyder (2012, Example 18.2) presents the case of a nonlinear constant elasticity demand curve and flat marginal cost curve, showing, for example, that monopoly shrinks consumer surplus to a degree commensurate with demand elasticity. At the extreme, as elasticity approaches infinity, monopoly causes a reduction in consumer surplus of

$1 - (1/e) = 0.6322\ldots$ or about 63 percent, with e Euler's constant.[19] By comparison, with a linear demand curve monopoly causes a 75 percent drop in consumer surplus. The fact that different specifications of the pure monopoly model generate different conclusions is important to keep in mind.[20]

2.4 APPLYING THE MODEL

The pure monopoly model is an insightful reference point when interpreting possible harm caused by monopoly and related anti-competitive phenomena. Government agencies, and courts, may refer to the pure monopoly model when determining if given market situation is offensively anti-competitive, offensive enough to break antitrust law. In this way, economic models can help to determine whether or not a business is guilty or liable for anti-competitive harm.

If antitrust guilt or liability is found, economic models may also help determine the form and extent of punishment and payments required of antitrust violators. The monetary loss to consumers from a monopoly overcharge on a quantity of goods purchased is the per-unit overcharge $P_m - P_c$ times the quantity Q_m sold. With P_m the monopoly price charged to customers, P_c is the benchmark price—whose value depends on some economic model. Earlier we interpreted P_c as the competitive equilibrium price and expressed overcharge in terms of demand and cost parameters via Eq. (2.8).

In the Sugar Trust case discussed earlier, market price is observed before and after a (near) monopoly takeover, and a relevant benchmark price is the "before" price, with no need to discern relevant values for demand and cost parameters when evaluating overcharge effects.[21]

Fines levied on an offending monopoly firm via the Sherman Act might be set equal to the monopolist's overcharge, assuming a benchmark price P_c can be determined.

Courts can award economic damages and relief to individuals, businesses, or society, in antitrust civil lawsuits against businesses, via the Clayton Act. The FTC government agency can prevent firms from merging or acquiring each other, via the FTC Act and Clayton Act.

2.5   MODEL'S LIMITATIONS AND EXTENSIONS

The pure monopoly model is an elegant and insightful simplification of the real world. It's likely not 100 percent accurate in any market situation. The most accurate "model" of any observable phenomenon is the phenomenon itself, but that "model" has no formal content or general theme. It's easy to add more realistic details to the pure monopoly model, much as one would add decals or stickers as a details on a model airplane. More substantively, the pure monopoly model can be modified to allow for fundamental departures from key underlying assumptions. This is like adding or switching parts on a model airplane.

Not every monopoly is well-described as "pure monopoly." The term itself appeared originally in Edward Chamberlain's book on monopolist competition (Chamberlain 1933), but appears earlier in Alfred Marshall's *Principles of Economics* (1890), and Marshall also sketches a variety of extensions to the model—to allow for efficiencies in the combining of firms, business goals other than short-term profit, and price discrimination.

In the sugar trust case (discussed earlier), the court concluded that the merged refineries were essentially a monopoly but cited market outcomes that cannot be explained in pure monopoly terms. Some possible scenarios in which monopolists might not overcharge and undersupply—in the way that pure monopolists do—are:

1. Efficiency: In becoming a monopolist, companies are merged and efficiencies gained, with higher productivity and lower marginal costs.
2. Competitive fringe: The monopolist cannot significantly overcharge without attracting competitors who enter the market, sell goods, and drive price toward its competitive equilibrium level.
3. Bad benchmark: The benchmark equilibrium market outcome in the pure monopoly is infeasible, making "overcharge" and "undersupply" irrelevant too.

Figure 2.3 depicts the "efficiency" scenario, #1 on the above list, with a big merger-induced drop in marginal cost (MC). The pre-merger competitive equilibrium, labeled E_c, has lower quantity and higher price than the post-merger monopoly equilibrium E_m. If the drop in marginal

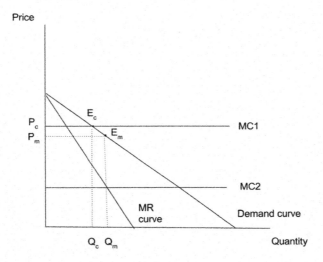

Fig. 2.3   Monopoly with merger efficiencies

cost is instead small, monopoly may end up lowering output and raising price,[22] like in the pure monopoly model.[23]

Example 2.3 In the US market for railroad passenger transportation, let the market demand curve be the straight line $P = 1000 - Q$. The marginal revenue curve is then a straight line $MR = 1000 - 2Q$. Let the marginal cost (MC) equal 800 for individual, competing firms, and let it be 400 for a monopoly firm. In competitive equilibrium, $MC = 800 = 1000 - Q$, and competitive quantity is $Q_c = 200$ and competitive price is $P_c = MC = 800$. In monopoly equilibrium, MC and MR curves cross: $MC = 400 = 1000 - 2Q$, so the monopolist's quantity is $Q_m = 300$ and their price is $P_m = 1000 - Q_m = 700$. So, the monopoly equilibrium provides more output, at a lower price, than competitive equilibrium. In terms of Marshallian surplus, monopoly and competition compare as in Table 2.2, with a gain in total surplus or welfare of 11,500.[24]

In the "competitive fringe" scenario, (#2, above), possible anti-competitive harm from a dominant firm is limited by free and willing entry of other firms into the market. It's possible that only one firm

Table 2.2   Surplus effects of pure monopoly

Equilibrium	Consumer surplus	Producer surplus	Total surplus
Monopoly	4500	9000	13,500
Competition	2000	0	2000
Difference	2500	9000	11,500

actually sells the good but charges a price that keeps economic profits close to zero, discouraging entry by other firms. In Fig. 2.1, the argument is that the monopoly firm will not go for pure monopoly outcome E_m because in doing so other firms will want some of the economic profits and enter the market, raising market quantity from Q_m toward Q_c.[25]

In the "bad benchmark" scenario (#3, above), competitive equilibrium—with many firms facing the same costs—is infeasible. To see how this scenario might play out, let competing firms each face a price P_c equal to the marginal cost MC of producing the good. Suppose, in addition, each firm faces a positive fixed setup cost F of getting into the business. Then economic profit of any one firm f—which is its revenue $P_c Q_f$ minus its total cost $F + MC \times Q_f$—is negative for each positive quantity Q_f it might produce. Assuming that firms refuse business opportunities that lose money, competitive equilibrium becomes infeasible and so irrelevant as a benchmark.[26]

2.6   PROBLEMS

1. In the pure monopoly model, two anti-competitive effects are a quantity drop and a price hike.
   (a) Which effect—quantity drop or price hike—seems to you the worse sort of anti-competitive effect on consumers? Explain.
   (b) Using Eqs. (2.6) and (2.7) in the text, for what values of the demand curve's slope parameter b is the quantity drop bigger (in absolute terms) than the price hike? For what values of b is the reverse true?
2. In the market for sugar, suppose that the market demand curve takes the form of the straight line $P = 10 - 2Q$, with price P on the vertical axis and quantity Q (in millions of pounds) on the horizontal axis. The

marginal revenue curve is then a straight line $MR = 10 - 4Q$. Let the marginal cost (MC) of producing a pound of sugar be 20 cents.

(a) Graph the demand curve, marginal revenue curve, and marginal cost curve, all on the same graph as in Fig. 3.1.

(b) Find the competitive equilibrium price and quantity, at which the demand curve and marginal cost curve intersect.

(c) Find the pure monopoly equilibrium quantity, at which the marginal revenue and marginal cost curves intersect, then find the monopoly price.

(d) Compare the competitive equilibrium and monopoly equilibrium outcomes, in terms of monopoly overcharge.

(e) Compute consumer surplus, producer surplus, and total surplus, in competitive equilibrium and monopoly equilibrium, similar to Example 2.1 in the text.

3. In the US market for high-performance personal computers, let the market demand curve be the straight line $P = 2000 - Q$. Let the marginal cost (MC) equal 1800 for individual, competing firms, and let it be 600 for a monopoly firm.

(a) Graph the demand curve, marginal revenue curve, and marginal cost curves, all on the same graph as in Fig. 3.2.

(b) Find the competitive equilibrium price and quantity, at which the demand curve and competitive marginal cost curve intersect.

(c) Find the monopoly equilibrium quantity, at which the marginal revenue curve and monopoly marginal cost curve intersect, and then find the monopoly price.

(d) Compare the competitive equilibrium and monopoly equilibrium outcomes, in terms of monopoly overcharge.

(e) Compute consumer surplus, producer surplus, and total surplus, in competitive equilibrium and monopoly equilibrium, similar to Example 2.3 in the text.

4. In an industry with a single seller and a competitive fringe of potential competitors, monopoly's extreme market concentration need not create anti-competitive effects. Explain.

5. In the market for computer operating systems, suppose that each firm that supplies systems faces a cost $F + MCQ$ of producing Q systems, with positive fixed cost F and marginal cost $MC = 2$. Suppose also that consumers' demand curve is $P = 3 - Q$.

(a) Find the competitive equilibrium quantity Q_c and price P_c, and show that industry profit $P_cQ_c - (F + MCQ_c)$ equals $-F$, which is negative. Will any firms choose to produce in this competitive industry? Explain.

(b) Find the monopoly equilibrium quantity Q_m and price P_m, and show that industry profit $P_m Q_m - (F + MC Q_m)$ equals $\frac{1}{4} - F$. If $F < \frac{1}{4}$, will the monopolist choose to produce in this industry? Explain.

6. Suppose that the demand curve for a good is: $P = \beta Q^{-1/\varepsilon}$, with β a positive parameter and ε the elasticity of demand—a number greater than 1. Firms produce the good with no fixed cost and with marginal cost MC which is the same for each unit produced.

(a) Show that the competitive equilibrium quantity is $Q_c = (MC/\beta)^{-\varepsilon}$, and competitive equilibrium price is MC.

(b) Suppose now that a monopoly takes over the industry. Show that the monopolist's marginal revenue is $MR = \beta(1 - \frac{1}{\varepsilon})Q^{-1/\varepsilon}$, and profit-maximizing quantity and price are $Q_m = \left(\frac{MC}{\beta(1-\frac{1}{\varepsilon})} \right)^{-\varepsilon}$, $P_m = \frac{MC}{1-\frac{1}{\varepsilon}}$.

(c) Show that the Lerner Index, defined as $(P - MC)/P$, equals 0 in competitive equilibrium and equals $1/\varepsilon$ in monopoly equilibrium.

(d) Show that $Q_m/Q_c = (1-\frac{1}{\varepsilon})^{\varepsilon}$ and $P_m/P_c = (1-\frac{1}{\varepsilon})^{-1}$, each increasing in ε. Does monopoly have anti-competitive effects on quantity and price? Explain.

(e) If $\varepsilon = 2$, show that monopoly causes price to double and quantity to fall by 75 percent.

(f) As elasticity ε approaches infinity, show that $P_m/P_c \to 1$ while $Q_m/Q_c \to 1/e$, with e Euler's constant. In the limit, does monopoly have anti-competitive effects? Explain.

NOTES

1. Being left-handed, and raised in Oregon, I know of no such company or way to make a left-handed back scratcher better than a regular back scratcher, but I beg the reader's indulgence.
2. Currently, Microsoft has a market share of about 90 percent.
3. This model appears in Marshall (1890) and was later termed "pure monopoly" – in contrast to pure or perfect competition – by Chamberlain (1933).

4. For retail sugar price data, see "Table 6—US retail refined sugar price, monthly, quarterly, and by calendar and fiscal year" provided by the USDA online, and for sugar quantity data, see USDA "Table 24a—US sugar: supply and use, by fiscal year."

5. Pure monopoly has the same consumer impact as the collusion of firms to fix price at a collectively profit-maximizing level, so pure monopoly is obviously bad for consumers. Schemes or agreements among firms that aim to fix prices, or limit price flexibility, can be declared illegal even without courts' reliance on market data, see *United States v. Trans-Missouri Freight Association,* 166 U.S. 290 (year 1897).

6. This classic text went through eight editions, you can browse/search the first online at babel.hathitrust.org, and download the last (8th) edition at libertyfund.ort.

7. Consumer surplus values equal areas of triangles framed by the demand curve/line and the price line. Producer surplus is zero in competitive equilibrium since there is an assumed constant marginal cost (MC) which coincides with the price line, while in monopoly equilibrium it is the area of the rectangle with (Q, P) corners $(0, 600), (0, 200), (100, 600), (100, 200)$, also equal to $(P_m - MC)Q_m$.

8. For values of Q greater than a/b, price is negative—impossible under usual circumstances.

9. With a flat marginal cost curve, a firm's total cost of producing a quantity Q is $F + MC \times Q$, with fixed cost F which here is assumed equal to zero. This sort of cost function is said to have constant returns.

10. A linear demand curve has constant slope and two parameters—an intercept and a slope. Another two parameter demand model is the constant elasticity model, which can be written $P = \beta Q^{-1/\varepsilon}$, with β positive and ε the elasticity of demand—assumed greater than 1. See discussion below and Problem 2.6 for more on this approach.

11. Demand and marginal cost curves cross at: $MC = P = a - bQ$, in which case $Q = (a - MC)/b$.

12. Revenue is $PQ = (a - bQ)Q$, and marginal revenue is $MR = d/dQ(PQ) = a - 2bQ$, in which case condition $MR = MC$ is the same as $a - 2bQ = MC$, yielding $Q_m = (a - MC)/(2b)$. Price is then $P_m = a - bQ_m = a - b((a - MC)/(2b))$, which is $(a + MC)/2$.

13. We can also express the quantity drop relative of initial (competitive) quantity, and likewise express price increase relative to initial price, the latter known as the Lerner Index: $(P_m - P_c)/P_c$ which here takes the form $((a/MC) - 1)/2$.

14. Consumer surplus, in competitive equilibrium = $(1/2)(a - P_c)Q_c$, which is $(1/2)(a - MC)((a - MC)/b)$, in turn equal to $(a - MC)^2/(2b)$. By comparison, in monopoly consumer surplus is $(1/2)(a - P_m)Q_m$, which is $(1/2)(a - (a +$

$MC)/2)(a-MC)/(2b)$, equal to $(1/2)((a-MC)/2)(a-MC)/(2b)$, also equal to $(a-MC)^2/(8b)$.

15. Producer surplus equal 0 in competitive equilibrium, while in monopoly it is $(P_m - MC)Q_m$, equal to $((a + MC)/2 - MC)(a - MC)/(2b)$, or just $(a - MC)^2/(4b)$.

16. Total surplus, in competition, is $(1/2)(a - MC)^2/(b)$, and in monopoly it is $(a - MC)^2/(8b)$ plus $(a - MC)^2/(4b)$, which is $(3/8)(a - MC)^2/b$.

17. Posner (1975) measures the social cost of monopoly as the deadweight loss $-\Delta TS$ plus the producer surplus increase ΔPS, which by definition equals the consumer surplus loss $-\Delta CS$ in going from competitive equilibrium to monopoly equilibrium. He shows empirically that such losses may be substantial in comparison to sales in industries like sugar, rubber, and electric bulbs.

18. For discussion see Whinston (2008, Chapter 1).

19. Equation (18.18) of Nicholson and Snyder (2012), with ε used here to denote demand elasticity in absolute (positive) terms, expresses the ratio of consumer surplus in monopoly and competition situations as $\frac{CS_m}{CS_c} = \left(\frac{1}{1-\frac{1}{\varepsilon}}\right)^{1-\varepsilon}$, and as ε approaches infinity this ratio approaches $1/e$, with e Euler's constant.

20. Which specifications are most appropriate, for drawing conclusions about actual markets, should be informed by data on buyers, sellers, and markets; see Posner (1975, 1976), for example.

21. For price-fixing, Section 15d of US Code Chap. 1 gives considerable leeway in the court's determination of economic damages: "...damages may be approved and assessed in the aggregate by statistical or sampling methods, by the computation of illegal overcharges, or by such other reasonable system of estimating aggregate damages as the court in its discretion may permit..."

22. Improved efficiency, and lower marginal cost, cannot rationalize the increased output *and* (slightly) higher price described in the sugar trust case. Some additional factor, such as increased sugar demand—and a shifting out of demand and marginal revenue curves—may also play a role.

23. See Williamson (1968) for a classic discussion of the tradeoffs involved in such cases.

24. As in Example 2.2, consumer surplus is the area of the triangle above the market price line and below the demand curve, while producer surplus is $Q_m(P - MC)$.

25. If each firm has identical costs—with the same marginal cost MC at each output level, and no fixed cost—then to discourage entry by fringe firms, the dominant firm will be forced to raise quantity to Q_c. If fixed cost is

instead positive, then fringe firms cannot enter the market costlessly, and the dominant firm need not raise quantity all the way to Q_c.

26. In this situation there the average cost of production is $(F+MC \times Q_f)/Q_f = F/Q_f + MC$, which is falling in Q_f. With decreasing average cost, the industry has increasing returns to scale, making monopoly a "natural" economic outcome. See Chap. 6 for more discussion of natural monopoly.

REFERENCES

Blair, R. D., & Kaserman, D. L. (2009). *Antitrust economics* (2nd ed.). New York: Oxford University Press.

Bork, R. H. (1977). *The antitrust paradox, a policy at war with itself.* New York, NY: Basic Books.

Chamberlain, E. H. (1933). *Theory of monopolistic competition.* Cambridge: Harvard University Press.

Marshall, A. (1890). *Principles of economics.* London: Macmillan.

Mas-Colell, A., Whinston, M. D., & Green, J. R. (1995). *Microeconomic theory.* New York: Oxford University Press Inc.

Nicholson, W., & Snyder, C. (2012). *Microeconomic theory: Basic principles and extenstions* (12th ed.). Boston: Cengage Learning.

Posner, R. A. (1975). The social costs of monopoly and regulation. *The Journal of Political Economy, 83*(4), 807–828.

Posner, R. (1976). *Antitrust law: An American perspective.* Chicago: The University of Chicago Press.

Whinston, M. D. (2008). *Lectures on antitrust economics.* Cambridge: The MIT Press.

Williamson, O. E. (1968). Economies as an antitrust defense: The welfare tradeoffs. *American Economic Review, 58*(1), 18–36.

PART II

Multi-Market Antitrust Economics

CHAPTER 3

Monopoly Spillover Effects

Abstract In a market that goes from many suppliers to just one supplier, the advent of monopoly has an immediate effect: change in supply in that market. The pure monopoly model, discussed in Chap. 2, represents the monopoly effect in a given market. The effect is anti-competitive: price rises above the many-supplier competitive level, and goods quantity falls, doubly bad for consumers. The simplicity of the pure monopoly model is a virtue but also limits the range of behavior and outcomes that can be discussed within it.

This chapter continues the discussion of monopoly effects, with a view beyond the market in which monopoly takes place. If a monopoly forms in a market for one good—call it good 1—and if price rises as the pure monopoly model predicts, then consumers may end up buying a different amount of another good, call it good 2, than they did before. In other words, the advent of monopoly in the market for good 1 may have "spillover effects" on the market for good 2. A study of such effects is worthwhile for its own sake and as a warm-up for studying mergers—see Chap. 4.

In this chapter, monopoly spillover effects are changes in consumption quantities of the second good, when the first good's market is monopolized. They can be positive, making consumers better off—or bad—making them worse off. These spillover effects are only part of the economic effect of monopoly, and regardless of whether spillovers are positive or negative, the total effect of monopoly on consumers is surely negative since it reduces their purchasing power.

The direction of monopoly spillover effects depends on the sense in which goods 1 and 2 are related in consumption terms. To keep track of spillovers, this chapter assumes that there are many sellers (and buyers) of good 2, and that its market is in competitive equilibrium. Also, for both goods it's assumed that producers' marginal cost of production doesn't change with production level, and that the consumers' demand curve is linear.

Under the assumptions made in this chapter, which extend those in Chap. 2, the extent and direction of monopoly spillover effects depends on consumers' preferences, as follows:

1. There are no monopoly spillover effects if goods 1 and 2 are unrelated or *independent*—meaning that a change in the price of one good has no effect on the demand for the other good.

2. There is a positive spillover effect, boosting consumption of good 2, if goods 1 and 2 are *substitutes*—meaning that an increase in the price of one good increases the demand for the other good. The percentage boost in good 2 quantity can rival the percentage decrease in good 1 quantity caused by monopoly. (If good 2 is something that the consumer likes less than good 1, substitution from the pricey monopolized good 1 to crummy good 2 constitutes a drop in goods quality and enjoyment for each additional unit of good 2 consumed, in which case the increase in good 2 consumption may be seen as a negative monopoly effect, not a positive one. But this negative effect is the net quality drop per unit of consumption across goods and is consistent with a positive consumption increase in good 2.)

3. There is a negative spillover effect, cutting consumption of good 2, if goods 1 and 2 are *complements*—meaning that an increase in the price of one good increases the demand for the other good. In percentage terms, the cut can rival that of good 1.

Any one good may have both substitutes and complements, and a convenient interpretation of the monopoly spillover effects presented here is that they may wash out: the good effects of substituting away from a monopolized good may be offset by the bad effects on reduced complement goods consumption. However, a similarly convenient interpretation of monopoly in a single market is that the anti-competitive effects of the monopolist's wedge between marginal revenue and marginal cost may be offset by efficiencies achieved by single-firm production. In each case there is merit in using data on firms, consumers, and markets to describe actual costs and benefits of monopoly, so long as such data is not too costly or onerous to get.

Keywords Monopoly • Complement • Substitute • Equilibrium • Spillover effect

3.1   INDEPENDENT GOODS

Let the demand curves for goods 1 and 2, respectively, be straight lines:

$$P_1 = a_1 - b_1 Q_1 \tag{3.1}$$

$$P_2 = a_2 - b_2 Q_2 \tag{3.2}$$

with positive parameters a_1, a_2, b_1, b_2 for which $a_1 > MC_1$ and $a_2 > MC_2$, with MC_1 the marginal cost of good 1 for each unit produced, and MC_2 the marginal cost of good 2 for each unit produced, and with quantities Q_1 in $(0, a_1/b_1)$ and Q_2 in $(0, a_2/b_2)$.

The demand curves (3.1)–(3.2) relate each good's price to its quantity. A change in P_1 does not change the demand curve for good 2, and likewise a change in P_2 does not change the demand curve for good 1. The two goods are independent, from the consumers' view. With this assumption, if a monopoly forms in the market for good 1, jacking up P_1, this does not change the demand for good 2. The outcome in market 2, assuming there are many buyers and sellers, is competitive equilibrium with price P_2 equal to marginal cost MC_2, and applying demand curve (3.2) equilibrium quantity solves $MC_2 = P_2 = a_2 - b_2 Q_2$, so $Q_2 = (a_2 - MC_2)/b_2$ which does not depend on what happens in market 1. Equilibrium price in market 2 is $a_2 - b_2 Q_2 = (a_2 + MC_2)/2$ which also doesn't depend on market 1. So, there are no spillover effects on market 2 of market 1 going from competition to monopoly, provided goods 1 and 2 are independent.

3.2   SUBSTITUTES

Consumers use some goods as substitutes for others, to a degree that depends the goods in question, as illustrated in Fig. 3.1.

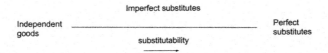

Fig. 3.1   Degree of substitution

Goods 1 and 2 are perfect substitutes if consumers are indifferent to replacing any unit of the first good with a unit of the second, in every consumption bundle they are presented with. From the consumer's perspective, the goods are identical, and in market equilibrium the goods must sell at the same price—consumers would refuse to buy good 1 if it were priced higher than good 2, and vice versa. If the market for good 2 is competitive, with price P_2 equal to marginal cost MC_2, then each unit of good 1 must also sell at that price: $P_1 = P_2 = MC_2$. If, in addition, the market for good 1 is competitive, then $P_1 = MC_1$, and the two industries must have the same marginal cost: $MC_1 = MC_2$. In this setting, a monopoly takeover of market 1 cannot raise price above marginal cost because consumers would stop buying good 1 and substitute fully into good 2, with all demand spilling over into that market.[1] In other words, if goods 1 and 2 are perfect substitutes and good 2's market is competitive, then there are neither direct nor spillover effects of monopoly in market 1.

Goods 1 and 2 are imperfect substitutes if they are not perfect substitutes yet the demand for one good rises with the price of the other—and vice versa, as in Fig. 3.2. For example, some consumers may consider hamburgers and hot dogs to be imperfect substitutes. Name-brand soda drinks, or name-brand blue jeans, are also possible examples of imperfect substitutes.

Each demand curve in Fig. 3.2 is a straight line, with formulas that appear below as numbered equations—for later reference:

$$P_1 = a_1 - b_1 Q_1 + c_1 P_2 \qquad (3.3)$$

$$P_2 = a_2 - b_2 Q_2 + c_2 P_1 \qquad (3.4)$$

with positive parameters $a_1, a_2, b_1, b_2, c_1, c_2$ for which $0 < c_1 < 1, 0 < c_2 < 1$, $a_1 + c_1 MC_2 > MC_1$ and $a_2 + c_2 MC_1 > MC_2$, and for quantities Q_1 in $(0, (a_1 - c_1 MC_2)/b_1)$ and Q_2 in $(0, (a_2 - c_2 MC_1)/b_2)$.

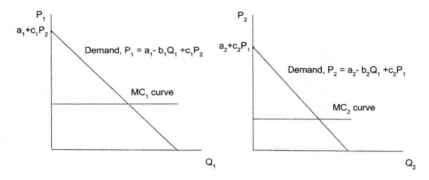

Fig. 3.2 Markets for two imperfect substitute goods

The parameter c_1 represents the effect of good 2's price change on the demand for good 1, and similarly c_2 represents the effect of good 1's price change on the demand for good 2. Positive values for these parameters imply that higher cross-market prices increase own-market demand. The assumption that $c_1 < 1$ and $c_2 < 1$ is natural for imperfect substitutes because the value 1 for each c parameter represents a perfect-substitute situation.[2]

Greater substitutability, in the model described here, means that the values of parameters c_1 and c_2 are higher, and this leads to a bigger quantity spillover effect on market 2 of monopoly formation in market 1. To see why, assume as earlier that the second market is in competitive equilibrium, with $P_2 = MC_2$. If the first market is also in competitive equilibrium, then competitive quantity and price are:

$$Q_{1c} = \frac{a_1 + c_1 MC_2 - MC_1}{b_1} \qquad (3.5)$$

$$P_{1c} = MC_1 \qquad (3.6)$$

If the first market instead has a monopoly with marginal revenue $MR_1 = a_1 - 2b_1 Q_1 + c_1 MC_2$ equal to marginal cost MC_1, then output and price are:

$$Q_{1m} = \frac{a_1 + c_1 MC_2 - MC_1}{2b_1} \qquad (3.7)$$

$$P_{1m} = \frac{a_1 + MC_1 + c_1 MC_2}{2} \tag{3.8}$$

In the market for good 2, quantity Q_2 is related to prices via the demand curve: $Q_2 = (a_2 + c_2 P_1 - P_2)/b_2$, and with $P_2 = MC_2$, quantity is $Q_2 = (a_2 + c_2 P_1 - MC_2)/b_2$. The effect on Q_2, of good 1's price rising from the competitive value MC_1 to the monopoly value $(a_1 + MC_1 + c_1 MC_2)/2$, is to increase Q_2 by the amount: $(c_2/b_2)(P_{1m} - P_{1c})$, which is a positive spillover effect:

$$\text{spillover effect} = \frac{c_2}{2b_2}(a_1 + c_1 MC_2 - MC_1). \tag{3.9}$$

With a_1 assumed greater than $c_1 MC_2 - MC_1$, the monopoly spillover effect on Q_2 is increasing in cross-price effect parameters c_1 and c_2.

In percentage terms, a shift from competition to monopoly in market 1 cuts quantity by 50 percent in that market, under the assumptions maintained here. The spillover effect on good 2 is to increase quantity by some percentage which depends on parameter values, but may be as high as 50 percent, as in the following example.

Example 3.1 Let the two industries be parameterized the same, with $a_1 = a_2$, $b_1 = b_2$, $c_1 = c_2$, and $MC_1 = MC_2$. With market 2 in perfect competition, and market 1 going from competition to monopoly, the market 2 quantity spillover effect (3.9) divided by initial market 2 quantity simplifies to $c_2/2$.[3] With c_2 in the range $(0,1)$, the spillover effect is an increase in good 2 in the 0 percent to 50 percent range.

The fact that the quantity increase for good 2 can rival the quantity decrease for good 1 fits the general description of monopoly as feat that can be pulled off only if there are no close substitutes for the target good— good 1 in this case. Positive spillover effects, on markets for substitutes, are generally expected.

Monopolization of industry 1 may have both quantity and price effects on other markets. However, under the assumption that industry 2 is in perfect competition equilibrium and firms' marginal cost MC_2 is the same for each unit produced, price P_2 equals MC_2 and is unaffected by monopolization of industry 1. For this reason, under the maintained assumptions "spillover effects" identified here include quantity effects but not price effects.[4]

3.3 COMPLEMENTS

For consumers, substitute goods don't go together—they are like repelling magnet ends—whereas complement goods do go together, like attracting magnet ends. If a monopoly forms in the market for good 1, and if good 2 is a complement for good 1, then there are anti-competitive spillover effects on the market for good 2: price goes up and quantity goes down. This is opposite the pro-competitive monopoly effects on substitute markets discussed earlier.

Just as there are perfect substitutes and imperfect ones, there are perfect and imperfect complements. With perfect complements the anti-competitive spillover effects of monopoly are starkest, and they fade as complementarity fades. The perfect complements case takes more explanation than the perfect substitutes one did earlier, and it gets its own Sect. 3.3.1 below, followed by Sect. 3.3.2 on imperfect complements.

3.3.1 Perfect Complements

Mergers across substitute goods industries can be anti-competitive, lowering goods quantity and raising price, with bigger effects when the goods are closer substitutes. Substitute goods are viewed by consumers as replacements for each other, while complement goods bear an opposite sort of relationship—being used together rather than instead of each other.

Perfect complements are goods that consumers prefer to use in some fixed proportions, like one hot dog to one bun. Quantities demanded, for perfect substitutes, are linearly related:

$$Q_2 = dQ_1 \tag{3.10}$$

for some positive number d, as in Fig. 3.3 where point A is a pair of quantities (Q_1, Q_2) that satisfies $Q_2 = dQ_1$. The dotted horizontal and vertical lines that meet A indicate that the consumer is indifferent between point A and any point on the dotted lines extending from A: in increase in good 1 only, or good 2 only, does not increase consumer welfare.

Given consumer preferences, if a consumer buys 1 unit of good, they will derive utility from it only by consuming it together with d units of good 2, and they would gain no additional utility from buying more than d units of good 2 per 1 unit of good 1. As such, they are unwilling to pay for any more than d units of good 2 per 1 unit of good 1, and will always

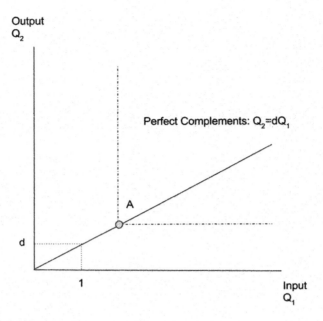

Fig. 3.3   Perfect complements

buy goods 1 and 2 as a package, with d units of good 2 for every 1 unit of good 1. Suppose that each quantity Q of the good bundle comes with $Q_1 = Q$ units of good 1 and $Q_2 = dQ$ units of good 2, and let demand for the bundled good be:

$$\text{goods bundle demand curve:} \quad P = a - bQ \tag{3.11}$$

for some positive numbers a and b and all Q in the range $(0, a/b)$.

Let goods 1 and 2 sell at prices P_1 and P_2, respectively. The cost of 1 unit of good 1 and d units of good 2 is $P_1 + dP_2$, this being the cost per unit of the consumer's bundle: $P = P_1 + dP_2$. From the bundle demand curve, $P = a - bQ$, and the quantity Q of bundles is the same as the quantity Q_1 of the first good consumed, in which case the demand for good 1 is:

$$P_1 = a - bQ_1 - dP_2 \tag{3.12}$$

for Q_1 in the range $(0, a - dP_2)/b$. Assuming that the market for good 2 is in competitive equilibrium, $P_2 = MC_2$ and for good 1 the competitive equilibrium quantity and price are:

$$Q_{1c} = \frac{a - MC_1 - dMC_2}{b} \tag{3.13}$$

$$P_{1c} = MC_1 \tag{3.14}$$

and the monopoly equilibrium price and quantity are:

$$Q_{1m} = \frac{a - MC_1 - dMC_2}{2b} \tag{3.15}$$

$$P_{1m} = \frac{a + MC_1 + dMC_2}{2} \tag{3.16}$$

With monopoly the quantity of good 1 provided drops by half, and since $Q_2 = dQ_1$, the quantity of good 2 also drops by half. That is, going from competition to monopoly in market 1 creates a negative spillover effect in market 2—a 50 percent drop in quantity consumed—the same percentage drop as for good 1. The change in the first quantity is, from Eqs. (3.13) and (3.15), $Q_{1m} - Q_{1c} = -dMC_2/(2b)$, in which case the change in the second good is d times that:

$$\text{spillover effect} = -\frac{d^2 MC_2}{2b} \tag{3.17}$$

which is larger when the amount d of good 2 that pairs with a unit of good 1 is larger, but remains a 50 percent drop in percentage terms.

3.3.2 Imperfect Complements

Negative spillover effects of monopoly across complement good markets are stark: goods quantity drops by half in the second market. The case of imperfect complements is less stark, but the same qualitatively. Goods 1 and 2 are imperfect complements if they are not perfect complements and if increase in the price of one good decreases the demand for the second good. Facing a price increase for good 1, if good 2 is an imperfect complement, the consumer will shy away from buying goods 1 and 2, lowering quantities of both goods. The idea is the same as with perfect complements, but the mechanics are somewhat different.

Demand curves, for imperfect complements, can be written in the same style as demand curves (3.3)–(3.4) for imperfect substitutes, but with the opposite sign for parameters c_1 and c_2. For imperfect complements, let c_1 and c_2 each be in the range $(-1,0)$, in which case an increase in P_2 shifts good 1's demand curve down by $c_1 P_2$ units, and an increase in P_1 shifts good 2's demand curve down by $c_2 P_1$ units. The closer are c_1 and c_2 to -1, the stronger is the goods complementarity.[5]

Earlier, the spillover effect of monopoly on an imperfect substitute's quantity appeared in Eq. (3.9), and was negative because the parameters c_1 and c_2 were assumed positive. Now, with c_1 and c_2 assumed negative, the same spillover formula (3.9) applies but the effect is positive rather than negative.

3.4   MODEL LIMITATIONS

As in Chap. 2, the conclusions of this chapter are limited by the restrictive nature of the models discussed. Aside from functional form restrictions on demand and cost curves, this chapter restricts the scope of "spillover effects" to cross-market changes in consumption quantity. Other possible effects include cross-market changes in price and profit: these are zero under the maintained assumption of a flat marginal cost curve but are not generally so if the marginal cost curve is increasing. Cross-market changes in consumer surplus are of interest, are a subject of ongoing research by the author.

A dissection of monopoly effects into two parts—direct and spillover effects—has some appeal but also masks the simultaneous nature of consumer choice in general equilibrium. Other issues of general equilibrium, like household labor income effects associated with monopoly formation, are also ignored here. Later in the book, Chaps. 5–6 discuss monopoly in relation to allied fields using basic general equilibrium models.[6]

3.5   PROBLEMS

1. In evaluating the effects of market concentration on consumers, do you think that spillover effects on consumption quantities in other markets are relevant? Why or why not?

2. If the market for cars were monopolized, name a second consumer market in which quantities purchased would rise, and a third in which the quantities purchased would fall.

3. In the US market for cane sugar, answer the following:
   (a) Using online sources, approximate the number of firms in the industry. Does the industry appear competitive? Why or why not.
   (b) Stevia, derived from the plant Stevia rebaudiana, is a substitute for cane sugar. Estimate its current price using online sources or via your grocery store. If the market for cane sugar were monopolized, by how much do you think the quantity consumed of Stevia would rise in percentage terms? Explain.
   (c) Eggs are a complement for cane sugar. Estimate their current price using online sources or via your grocery store. If the market for cane sugar were monopolized, by how much do you think the quantity consumed of eggs would fall in percentage terms? Explain.

4. Suppose that polo shirts and t-shirts are substitute goods, with good 1 being polo shirts and good 2 being t-shirts. Suppose that the demand curve for good 1 is $P_1 = 3 - Q_1 - 0.5P_2$, and the demand good for t-shirts is $P_2 = 2 - Q_2 - 0.5P_1$. Also, suppose the marginal cost of producing a polo shirt is $MC_1 = 2$, and the marginal cost of producing a t-shirt is $MC_2 = 1$.
   (a) Find the competitive equilibrium values of polo shirt quantity and price, and t-shirt quantity and price.
   (b) Find the monopoly equilibrium value of polo shirt quantity and price, assuming the t-shirt market is competitive.
   (c) Find the spillover effect of polo shirt monopoly on t-shirt consumption. Is it a big effect? Explain.

5. Suppose that polo shirts and shorts are complement goods, with good 1 being polo shirts and good 2 being shorts. Suppose that the demand curve for good 1 is $P_1 = 3 - Q_1 + 0.5P_2$, and the demand good for shorts is $P_2 = 3 - Q_1 + 0.5P_1$. Also, suppose the marginal cost of producing a polo shirt or pair of shorts is $MC_1 = MC_2 = 2$.
   (a) Find the competitive equilibrium values of polo shirt quantity and price, and shorts quantity and price.
   (b) Find the monopoly equilibrium value of polo shirt quantity and price, assuming the shorts market is competitive.
   (c) Find the spillover effect of polo shirt monopoly on shorts consumption. Is it a big effect? Explain.

6. Suppose that all consumers have identical preferences for goods and that the representative consumer has income I and chooses consumption amounts Q_1 and Q_2 of goods 1 and 2, subject to prices P_1 and P_2 via the budget constraint: $P_1Q_1 + P_2Q_2 = I$. The consumer's utility of consumption takes the form of a Cobb-Douglas utility function: $u(Q_1, Q_2) = Q_1^\theta Q_2^{1-\theta}$, with θ a parameter whose value lies in the range $(0, 1)$.

   (a) Show that the consumer's utility-maximizing choice of consumption quantities is $Q_1 = \frac{\theta I}{P_1}$ and $Q_2 = \frac{(1-\theta)I}{P_2}$.

   (b) With market demand curves $P_1 = \frac{\theta I}{Q_1}$ and $P_2 \frac{(1-\theta)}{Q_2}$ for goods 1 and 2, the curves are price-quantity relationships. Are goods 1 and 2 independent, substitutes, or complements?

NOTES

1. If marginal cost is less for good 1 than good 2, a monopoly in market 1 may lead to equal prices for goods 1 and 2, whereas competition in both markets would mean no demand for good 2. Here the monopoly spillover effect would be to create some market for good 2.

2. If $c_1 = c_2 = 1$ then, from the demand curves (3.3)–(3.4), $P_1 - P_2 = a_1 - b_1 Q_1$ and $P_2 - P_1 = a_2 - b_2 Q_2$. so $a_1 - b_1 Q_1 = -(a_2 - b_2 Q_2)$, and $Q_2 = (a_1 + a_2) - (b_1/b_2)Q_1$, in which case there is a negative linear relationship between Q_1 and Q_2.

3. The spillover effect $(c_2/(2b_2))(a_1 + c_1 MC_2 - MC_1)$ divided by initial quantity $Q_2 = (a_2 + c_2 MC_1 - MC_2)/b_2$ is, with same parameterization in the two markets, equal to $(c_1/(2b_1))(a_1 + c_1 MC_1 - MC_1)$ divided by $(a_1 + c_1 MC_1 - MC_1)/b_1$, which simplifies to c_2.

4. If instead marginal cost MC_2 is increasing in Q_2, then both price and quantity may rise in response to monopolization of industry 1.

5. If $c_1 = c_2 = -1$ then, from the demand curves (3.3)–(3.4), $P_1 + P_2 = a_1 - b_1 Q_1$ and also $P_2 + P_1 = a_2 - b_2 Q_2$, in which case quantities have a positive linear relationship: $Q_2 = (a_2 - a_1)/b_2 + (b_1/b_2)Q_1$ which is perfect complementarity—though in a more general sense than stated earlier since Q_2 can be positive even if Q_1 is zero, unless $a_1 = a_2$.

6. For more on the economic foundations of monopoly and markets see Lerner (1934), Posner (1975, 1976), and Tullock (1967).

REFERENCES

Lerner, A. P. (1934). The concept of monopoly and the measurement of monopoly power. *Review of Economic Studies, 1*(3), 157–175.

Posner, R. (1975). The social costs of monopoly and regulation. *Journal of Political Economy, 83*(4), 807–828.

Posner, R. (1976). *Antitrust law: An American perspective.* Chicago: The University of Chicago Press.

Tullock, G. (1967). The welfare costs of tariffs, monopolies, and theft. *Western Economic Journal, 5,* 224–232.

CHAPTER 4

Mergers

Abstract Mergers between firms can have anti-competitive consequences, to a degree that depends on the number of merging firms and on the industries in which the firms operate. If the firms are in the same industry, and if there are many that merge into one firm, the situation is like going from pure competition to pure monopoly, with starkly anti-competitive effects—see Chap. 2 for discussion. If there are few firms in an industry to start with, merging few into one is less dramatic than merging many to one, and merger effects may be less severe.

If firms are merging across industries, the firms' pursuit of profit maximization pre- and post-merger can produce merger effects on equilibrium quantity and price in each industry. The direction of these effects—up or down—depends on how goods are related to each other in terms of consumption or production. Generally, results depend on whether the goods are independent, substitutes, complements, or vertically linked.

This chapter discusses merger effects within a consumer goods industry and also across consumer goods industries, extending the simple static modeling approach of Chaps. 2 and 3 to allow for basic strategic interaction between two merging firms. Topics include horizontal mergers, conglomerate mergers, market extension mergers, and vertical mergers.

Keywords Merger • Horizontal merger • Vertical merger • Conglomerate merger • Independent goods

© The Author(s) 2018   51
S. Gilbert, *Multi-Market Antitrust Economics*, Quantitative
Perspectives on Behavioral Economics and Finance,
https://doi.org/10.1007/978-3-319-69386-6_4

4.1   Mergers in the Same Industry

Applying the principles of pure monopoly and perfect competition from Chap. 2, consider a merger—or merging—of all the firms in a single competitive market, into a single monopoly firm. With all firms providing the same good in the same market, this is the simplest form of a horizontal merger.[1]

The market effect, as described earlier, is to reduce output and raise price, unless merging allows for efficiencies and cost reductions. With perfect competition representing a market with 0 concentration of market power within any given firm, monopoly represents a market with 100 percent concentration of market power within a single firm.

A less extreme form of market concentration is duopoly, with two sellers in the marketplace. If the two sellers face identical costs, the duopoly outcome will have each selling half of all goods in the marketplace, and market concentration will be at 50 percent. Monopoly, duopoly, and perfect competition are each forms of industrial organization, and a merger could take a market from competition to either duopoly or monopoly, or from duopoly to monopoly.

To describe merger effects on a single market, let the demand curve in the market be linear, as in Eq. (2.1) in Chap. 2 and restated for convenience as Eq. (4.1) below:

$$P = a - bQ \qquad (4.1)$$

with a the buyers' maximum willingness to pay, and b the increase in price that induces a 1 unit decrease in quantity demanded. For firms, assume zero fixed cost and the same marginal cost value MC for each additional unit produced, with MC less than a.

Like the pure monopoly model, the duopoly model assumes that firms maximize profits. In duopoly there are two firms, the first supplying output Q_1 and the second supplying Q_2. Total output is then $Q = Q_1 + Q_2$. Firm 1 profit is is $PQ_1 - MC_1$, and applying the demand curve (4.1) to Q_1, profit is $(a - b(Q_1 + Q_2))Q_1 - MCQ_1$. Similarly firm 2 profit is $(a - b(Q_1 + Q_2))Q_2 - MCQ_2$.

Suppose that each firm seeks to maximize profit by choosing the quantity of good to sell, conditional on the quantity that the other firm will sell. This is called the Cournot model of duopoly, and the resulting equilibrium is called Cournot equilibrium or Cournot-Nash equilibrium.[2] The first firm maximizes profit by setting to zero the derivative of its profit with respect to Q_1:

$$a - bQ_2 - 2bQ_1 - MC = 0 \qquad (4.2)$$

and similarly the second firm sets to zero the derivative of its profit with respect to Q_2:

$$a - bQ_1 - 2bQ_2 - MC = 0 \qquad (4.3)$$

The pair of Eqs. (4.2)–(4.3) involves two variables Q_1 and Q_2, which can be solved by substitution from one equation to the other, or via matrix algebra, with solution:

$$Q_1 = Q_2 = \frac{a - MC}{3b} \qquad (4.4)$$

Market output $Q = Q_1 + Q_2$ and price P are then:

$$Q = \frac{2(a - MC)}{3b}, \qquad (4.5)$$

$$P = \frac{1}{3}a + \frac{2}{3}MC. \qquad (4.6)$$

For comparison to competitive equilibrium and pure monopoly equilibrium outcomes, Table 4.1 shows the equilibrium quantity and price in the pure or perfect competition, pure duopoly, and pure monopoly cases, using the notation a and b for the demand curve's parameters.[3]

With a linear demand curve and constant marginal cost, the effect of merging many competing companies to one company is to cut quantity Q in half and raise price P from marginal cost (MC) to the midpoint of

Table 4.1 Market concentration and outcomes

Industrial organization	Quantity	Price	Market concentration
Competition	$\frac{a-MC}{b}$	MC	0
Duopoly	$\frac{2}{3}\frac{a-MC}{b}$	$\frac{1}{3}a + \frac{2}{3}MC$	50
Monopoly	$\frac{1}{2}\frac{a-MC}{b}$	$\frac{1}{2}a + \frac{1}{2}MC$	100

MC and the buyers' maximum willingness to pay a. The effect of merging many companies into two companies (duopoly) is milder, as is the effect of merging two companies into one. In each case, mergers lower quantity and raise price, making consumers worse off.

Example 4.1 Let the market be for railroad passenger transportation, with demand curve $P = 1000 - Q$. Let the marginal cost (MC) equal 400 for individual (duopoly) firms, and let also it be 400 for a merged (monopoly) firm. Applying the formulas in Table 4.1, in duopoly equilibrium quantity is 400 and price is 600, while in monopoly equilibrium quantity is 300 and price is 700. A merger of the two duopoly firms, into monopoly, lowers quantity by 100 and raises price by the same amount.

Mergers may be anti-competitive, or instead increase firms' efficiency and lower their costs. In the case of many competitive firms merging into a monopoly, Chap. 2 discussed how cost cuts could lead a monopoly to raise output and lower price. Similarly, a merger of two duopoly firms into a monopoly may afford cost cuts and benefits to consumers, as in the following example.

Example 4.2 Let the market be for railroad passenger transportation, as in Example 4.1, with demand curve $P = 1000 - Q$. Let the marginal cost (MC) equal 700 for individual duopoly firms, and let it be 400 for a monopoly firm. Applying Table 4.1, in duopoly equilibrium quantity is 200 and price is 800, while in monopoly equilibrium quantity is 300 and price is 700. A merger of the two duopoly firms, into monopoly, raises quantity by 100 and lowers price by the same amount.

Absent efficiencies or cost savings, mergers in the same industry are anti-competitive, lowering quantity and raising price. The discussion here assumes linear demand curves, flat marginal cost curves, and firms duopoly competition via profit-maximizing quantity choice—conditional on the other firm's choice. There are many variants of this basic horizontal merger model. For example, each duopolist may choose a profit-maximizing price—conditional on the other firm's price—reaching the duopoly's Bertrand equilibrium. In Bertrand equilibrium, if the first firm sets price above marginal cost, then the second firm will optimally choose to undercut that price, while remaining above marginal cost, thereby grabbing all the business and profit. The second firm has similar motives, and the result is that Bertrand equilibrium price equals marginal cost—precluding the undercut—and the market outcome is the same as competitive equilibrium. If the two firms merge, and the merged firm chooses price to maximize profit, the outcome is as though it chooses quantity to maximize profit—each a monotonic function of the other via the demand curve. So, the merged-firm monopoly behaves the same in either case. As a result, anti-competitive effects of merging from Bertrand duopoly to monopoly are bigger than the effects of merging from Cournot duopoly to monopoly.[4]

Demand curve linearity and marginal cost curve flatness are assumed here or simplicity, but the anti-competitive nature of pure horizontal mergers holds more generally; see Farrell and Shapiro (1990).[5] Common to Cournot and Bertrand duopoly is a static equilibrium, and an alternative is dynamic or inter-temporal firm strategies, via "repeated games" and "learning" models. These models exceed the scope of this book, but are covered extensively in the literature on industrial organization—see xxx and yyy.

4.2 CONGLOMERATE MERGERS

A merger of firms in the same industry increases market concentration and, absent efficiencies from combining firms, provides consumers fewer goods at higher prices. Firms in different industries may merge, and the consequences for consumers of such a merger depend on the relationship between the goods.

Consider a merger or acquisition among two firms, each producing a consumer good, with the goods are unrelated or independent from the perspective of the consumer, meaning that a change in the price of one of the goods has no effect on consumer demand for the other good. Such a merger is called a conglomerate merger. There is no obvious reason why a conglomerate merger would affect equilibrium price or quantity in either of the good's markets, and the oft-cited rationale for such mergers is diversification rather than economic profit.[6]

For independent goods, a change in the price of the first good may change consumers' spending on that good, but doesn't change their spending on the second one. Whether or not any two goods are independent, in this sense, depends on what the consumer uses them for, and on the consumer's satisfaction or utility from consuming them. An example might be books and groceries: if book prices fall due to a growing online supply, consumers may buy more books but not necessarily change their grocery purchases.

To describe a merger or acquisition across independent goods' industries, suppose that the demand curves in the two industries are straight lines relating own-price to own-quantity, as in Eqs. (3.1) and (3.2) from Chap. 3. In each industry, suppose there is a single profit-maximizing firm with a marginal cost MC_1 in industry 1 and MC_2 in industry 2.

If the two firms merge, they form a single company that chooses both Q_1 and Q_2 to maximize the combined profit for the two industries. The combined profit is the sum of profits in the two industries. Cost in the first industry is $MC_1 Q_1$, and $MC_2 Q_2$ in the second industry. Then combined or merged profit is total revenue minus total cost:

$$\text{merged profit:} \quad P_1 Q_1 + P_2 Q_2 - MC_1 Q_1 - MC_2 Q_2 \qquad (4.7)$$

with price P_1 depending on Q_1 but not Q_2, and price P_2 depending on Q_2 but not Q_1. Since Q_2 does not affect profit in the first industry, and Q_1 does not affect profit in the second industry, the merged firm's choice of Q_1 is the same as the first firm's pre-merger choice. Likewise the post-merger choice of Q_2 is the same as the pre-merger choice.[7] In other words, in this model a merger of firms in independent industries changes neither price nor quantity in any industry, so does not affect consumers.

Example 4.3 Let demand curves take the form $P_1 = 10 - Q_1$ and $P_2 = 10 - Q_2$, let marginal cost in each industry be $MC = 8$. Figure 4.1 shows the demand and marginal cost curves.

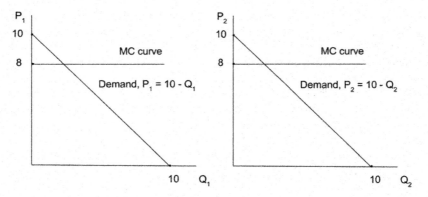

Fig. 4.1   Markets for two independent goods

Pre-merger, for each of the two firms $i = 1, 2$ profit takes the form $P_i Q_i - MC Q_i$, in which case:

$$\text{profit}_i = (10 - Q_i)Q_i - 8Q_i,$$

To maximize profit, firm i sets the derivative of its profit function equal to zero: $10 - 2Q_i - MC = 0$, in which case $Q_i = (10 - 8)/2 = 1$ and $P_i = 5 + MC/2 = 5 + 8/2 = 9$.

Post-merger, the merged firm choose quantities Q_1 and Q_2 so as to maximize combined profit: profit = $\text{profit}_1 + \text{profit}_2$, this being:

$$\text{profit} = (10 - Q_1)Q_1 + (10 - Q_2)Q_2 - 8Q_1 - 8Q_2. \tag{4.8}$$

To find the merged firm's profit-maximizing choice of Q_1, we can take the derivative of profit—in formula (4.8)—with respect to Q_1. That yields the same choice $Q_1 = 1$ as the pre-merger profit-maximizing monopolist made, and similarly Q_2 is the same pre- and post-merger.

To illustrate, consider a merger between online retail giant Amazon.com and high-end grocery store chain Whole Foods. Such a merger has recently been proposed, and raises no obvious concerns of anti-competitive harm, at least not from the standpoint of basic economic theory, since consumers arguably consider goods bought online from Amazon.com largely independent of groceries bought from Whole Foods. Whether or not consumers actually consider these two types of goods to be independent must be tested rather than merely assumed, and there may be some dynamic strategies at play that could make the proposed merger ultimately anti-competitive, but absent such considerations there are appears little cause for the Federal Trade Commission (FTC), US Department of Justice (DOJ), or competing firms to take antitrust issue with the proposed merger.

4.3 MERGERS ACROSS SUBSTITUTE GOODS

Horizontal mergers involve firms providing the same or similar goods. Section 4.1 discussed the case where firms provide the same good. In this case any two units of good within an industry are identical from the consumer's perspective, and so are perfect substitutes and sell at the same price.[8]

Figure 3.1, in Chap. 3, provides a hint about the possible market effects of a merger across industries for goods that are imperfect substitutes.

At the extreme of no substitutability—independent goods—there are no market effects of a merger, while at the extreme of perfect substitutability, a merger reduces quantity and raises price, to the extent that would happen if the goods were the same and included in a single market. In between, a merger plausibly reduces quantity and raises price—to a degree that increases with the degree of goods' substitutability. If so, anti-competitive merger effects weaken as the degree of substitutability weakens.

To analyze merger effects across markets for imperfect substitutes, let the two substitute goods have demand curves—relating a given good's price to that good's quantity demanded and the other good's price—that are linear as in Eqs. (3.3)–(3.4) from Chap. 3. Suppose that each firm maximizes profit by choosing a quantity to produce, given the quantity chosen by the other firm. To find the resulting Cournot duopoly equilibrium, it's useful to first solve for prices in terms of quantities, via substitution from (3.3) into (3.4) or vice versa, or via matrix algebra, yielding:

$$P_1 = \frac{a_1 + c_1 a_2 - b_1 Q_1 - b_2 c_1 Q_2}{1 - c_1 c_2}, \tag{4.9}$$

$$P_2 = \frac{a_2 + c_2 a_1 - b_2 Q_2 - b_1 c_2 Q_1}{1 - c_1 c_2}. \tag{4.10}$$

With prices expressed in terms of quantities, firm 1's profit takes the form $P_1(Q_1, Q_2)Q_1 - MC_1 Q_1$, and firm 2's profit takes the form $P_2(Q_1, Q_2)Q_2 - MC_2 Q_2$, with $P_1(Q_1, Q_2)$ the function in (4.9) and $P_2(Q_1, Q_2)$ in (4.10).

To maximize profit, firm 1 takes the derivative of its profit with respect to good 1 and sets it equal to 0, yielding a first-order necessary condition, and firm 2 acts analogously, yielding a second first-order condition, the pair of them as follows:

$$2b_1 Q_1 + b_2 c_1 Q_2 = a_1 + a_2 c_1 - (1 - c_1 c_2) MC_1, \tag{4.11}$$

$$2b_2 Q_2 + b_1 c_2 Q_1 = a_2 + a_1 c_2 - (1 - c_1 c_2) MC_2. \tag{4.12}$$

Solving these two equations for Q_1 and Q_2 yields the Cournot duopoly quantities Q_{d1} and Q_{d2}.[9]

With a merger, the merged firm maximizes combined profits from both firms: $(P_1(Q_1, Q_2) - MC_1)Q_1 + (P_2(Q_1, Q_2) - MC_2)Q_2$, and the necessary first-order conditions for a maximum are[10]:

$$2b_1Q_1 + (b_1c_2 + b_2c_1)Q_2 = a_1 + a_2c_1 - (1 - c_1c_2)MC_1, \quad (4.13)$$

$$2b_2Q_2 + (b_1c_2 + b_2c_1)Q_1 = a_2 + a_1c_2 - (1 - c_1c_2)MC_2. \quad (4.14)$$

Solutions for pre-merger and post-merger equilibrium quantities are somewhat complicated functions of underlying parameters. If $c_1 = c_2 = 0$, then the pre-merger and post-merger quantities of good 1 are the same, as are the quantities of good 2, each equal to the pure monopoly equilibrium quantity that arises in the absence of substitution.[11] Hausman et al. (2011) provide analysis of the post-merger equilibrium in more general terms, and related details are the subject of current research by the author of this book. The situation simplifies a lot if firms are assumed to be identical in terms of demand and cost curves, and that's the approach taken here.

Suppose that parameter values are the same across industries, and denote $a = a_1 = a_2$, $b = b_1 = b_2$, $c = c_1 = c_2$, and $MC = MC_1 = MC_2$. The solution for pre- and post-merger profit-maximizing quantities, in this case, is[12]:

$$Q_{d1} = Q_{d2} = \left(\frac{1+c}{2+c}\right)\frac{a - MC(1-c)}{b}, \quad (4.15)$$

$$Q_{r1} = Q_{r2} = \left(\frac{1}{2}\right)\frac{a - MC(1-c)}{b}. \quad (4.16)$$

The merger decreases equilibrium quantities, as can be seen by comparing quantities in Eqs. (4.15) and (4.16), with the ratio of Q_{ri} to Q_{di} being:

$$\frac{Q_{ri}}{Q_{di}} = \frac{2+c}{2+2c}, \quad (4.17)$$

for firms $i = 1, 2$, each ratio in the range $(0, 1)$ since c is positive. As c approaches 0, which is the case of independent goods, the quantity ratio approaches 1. As c approaches 1, which is a case of perfect substitutes, the quantity ratio approaches 3/4, and this matches the contrast between pure Cournot duopoly quantity and monopoly quantity in Table 4.1 in Sect. 4.3.

With prices related negatively to quantities via (4.9)–(4.10), the merger also increases equilibrium prices, and so has anti-competitive effects on both quantity and price. Applying (4.15)–(4.16) to (4.9)–(4.10), the equilibrium pre- and post-merger prices are:

$$P_{d1} = P_{d2} = \left(\frac{1}{1-c} - \frac{1}{2+c}\right)a + \left(\frac{1-c}{2+c}\right)MC. \tag{4.18}$$

$$P_1 = P_{r2} = \left(\frac{1}{1-c} - \frac{1}{2(1+c)}\right)a + \left(\frac{1-c}{2(1+c)}\right)MC. \tag{4.19}$$

Example 4.4 Let $a = 10$, $b = 1$, and $c = 1/2$. Applying (4.9)–(4.10), prices relate to quantities via:

$P_1 = 20 - \frac{4}{3}Q_1 - \frac{2}{3}Q_2,$
$P_2 = 20 - \frac{2}{3}Q_1 - \frac{4}{3}Q_2.$

Pre-merger, firms' profit are:

$$\text{profit}_1 = \left(20 - \frac{4}{3}Q_1 - \frac{2}{3}Q_2\right)Q_1 - MCQ_1$$

$$\text{profit}_2 = \left(20 - \frac{4}{3}Q_2 - \frac{2}{3}Q_1\right)Q_2 - MCQ_2$$

Each firm maximizes profit at that quantity at which marginal profit equals 0, in which case:

$$20 - \frac{8}{3}Q_1 - \frac{2}{3}Q_2 - MC = 0$$

$$20 - \frac{8}{3}Q_2 - \frac{2}{3}Q_1 - MC = 0$$

and so[13,14]:

$$Q_1 = Q_2 = 6 - \frac{3}{10}MC,$$

$$P_1 = P_2 = 8 + (3/5)MC.$$

The merged firm chooses Q_1 and Q_2 to maximize profit $P_1Q_1 - P_2Q_2 - (MCQ_1 + MCQ_2)$, with prices P_1 and P_2 determined by demand, in which case:

$$\text{profit} = \left(20 - \frac{4}{3}Q_1 - \frac{2}{3}Q_2\right)Q_1 + \left(20 - \frac{4}{3}Q_2 - \frac{2}{3}Q_1\right)Q_2 - MC(Q_1 + Q_2).$$

The firm maximizes profit by taking derivative with respect to Q_1 and Q_2, and setting each derivative to zero:

$$20 - \frac{8}{3}Q_1 - \frac{4}{3}Q_2 - MC = 0$$

$$20 - \frac{8}{3}Q_2 - \frac{4}{3}Q_1 - MC = 0$$

the solution being[15,16]:

$$Q_1 = Q_2 = 5 - \frac{1}{4}MC$$

$$P_1 = P_2 = 10 + (1/2)MC$$

Table 4.2 shows price and quantity differences, pre- and post-merger, and inspecting the bottom row of the table, since $MC < a = 10$, it follows that post-merger quantity has fallen and price has risen. In the case $MC = 8$, Table 4.3 shows the pre- and post-merger price and quantity.

Table 4.2 Merger across substitutes

Merger Pre or post?	Good 1 Quantity	Price	Good 2 Quantity	Price
Pre	$6 - \frac{3}{10}MC$	$8 + \frac{3}{5}MC$	$6 - \frac{3}{10}MC$	$8 + \frac{3}{5}MC$
Post	$5 - \frac{1}{4}MC$	$10 + \frac{1}{2}MC$	$5 - \frac{1}{4}MC$	$10 + \frac{1}{2}MC$
Post-pre	$-1 - \frac{1}{20}MC$	$2 - \frac{1}{10}MC$	$-1 - \frac{1}{20}MC$	$2 - \frac{1}{10}MC$

Table 4.3   Numerical illustration, substitutes merger

Merger Pre or post?	Good 1 Quantity	Price	Good 2 Quantity	Price
Pre	16/5	64/5	16/5	64/5
Post	3	14	3	14
Post-pre	−7/5	6/5	−7/5	6/5

Example 4.2 illustrates the anti-competitive effect of a cross-industry substitutes merger, with industry demand and cost parameterized identically in the two industries. As discussed earlier, such horizontal mergers reduce quantity and raise price for other parameter values, so long as they are the same for each industry. As in Sect. 4.3, the assumption that duopoly competing firms choose quantities—in Cournot fashion—can be replaced by the assumption that they choose prices, in Bertrand fashion; with the result that, once again, horizontal mergers are anti-competitive.[17]

4.4   COMPLEMENT GOODS

Consider two industries, with the good produced in industry 1 a complement of the good in industry 2, in the sense discussion in Chap. 3. A merger of firms, across complement goods markets, is sometimes called a market extension merger. The competition effects of such mergers are generally different than those of mergers across substitute goods markets, and in the simple models discussed here, mergers across complements are pro-competitive—raising quantities and lowering prices— while mergers across substitutes are anti-competitive, lowering quantities and raising prices.

4.4.1   Perfect Complements

Suppose that goods 1 and 2 are perfect complements in the sense discussed in Chap. 3: for each additional unit of good 1, the consumer must have at least d units of good 2 to achieve any utility from the additional unit of good 1, with any additional amounts of good 2 providing no extra utility.

Consider consumption bundles which consist of 1 unit of good 1 and d units of good 2. The price P of a consumption bundle is $P = P_1 + dP_2$. Let the demand curve for consumption bundles be:

$$P = a - bQ \qquad (4.20)$$

with positive parameters a and b, and Q the quantity of consumption bundles, assumed to be in the range $(0, a/b)$. Let the marginal cost of producing a given unit of good 1 be MC_1, and that of good 2 be MC_2, and suppose that $a > MC$ with bundle marginal cost $MC = MC_1 + dMC_2$. Also, suppose there are no fixed costs.

Let there be a single firm that produces good 1, and a single firm that produces good 2. If the firms 1 and 2 merge, producing an amount of bundled good Q so as to maximize profit $PQ - MCQ$, with price $P = a - bQ$, marginal cost $MC = MC_1 + dMC_2$, and no fixed cost. The profit-maximizing quantity is:

$$Q = \frac{a - (MC_1 + dMC_2)}{2b}, \qquad (4.21)$$

and since $Q_1 = Q$ and $Q_2 = Q/d$, the post-merger profit-maximizing merged-company quantities of goods 1 and 2 are:

$$Q_{r1} = \frac{1}{2b}(a - (MC_1 + dMC_2)) \qquad (4.22)$$

$$Q_{r2} = \frac{d}{2b}(a - (MC_1 + dMC_2)) \qquad (4.23)$$

These post-merger quantities are twice the corresponding pre-merger quantities. The price of the bundled good is $P = a - bQ$, and plugging in the Q formula yields post-merger bundle merged-company price:

$$P_r = \frac{1}{2}(a + MC_1 + dMC_2) \qquad (4.24)$$

With $P = P_1 + dP_2$, the firm and the consumers are each indifferent to the value of prices P_1 and P_2, so long as $P = P_1 + dP_2$. In this sense, post-merger prices for each individual good are indeterminant.

Now consider the pre-merger situation where firm 1 and firm 2 individually make choices so as to maximize profit, conditional on the choice made by the other firm. Whatever may be the pre-merger outcome, the pre-merger prices cannot be compared to post-merger prices market by market because post-merger prices are indeterminant. It may be possible to compare bundle prices P pre- and post-merger, and market-specific quantities, but even that can be hard. To illustrate, suppose that the idea is that each firm will pick a production quantity, conditional on the observed quantity of the other firm. Firm 1 picks Q_1, having observed Q_2, and vice versa. Firm 1's profit is $(P_1 - MC_1)Q_1$, with $P_1 = a + bQ_1 - dP_2$, in which case profit is $(a + bQ_1 - dP_2 - MC_1)Q_1$. Firm 1 is assumed to observe Q_2, when trying to maximize profit, but knowing Q_2 doesn't tell firm 1 the cross-market price P_2 upon which firm 1's profit depends. Cross-market price and quantity are related via $P_1 + dP2 = a + bQ_2$, and so $P_2 = ((a + bQ_2/d) - P_1)/d$, but this depends on P_1. Firm 1 is unable to frame the profit as a known function of its quantity choice variable, and the same is true of firm 2, making the pre-merger profit-maximizing market outcome undefined.

With a partly indeterminant post-merger profit-maximizing outcome, and a possibly undefined pre-merger profit-maximizing outcome, the market effect of a merger across perfect complements is possibly undefined. This trouble spot, in merger modeling, cannot be fixed but can be explored from other angles. At the least, one can say that the foregoing discussion identifies no bad effects of mergers across perfect complement markets, a conclusion generally consistent with the literature on the subject.

With some variation in the approach to modeling perfect complement mergers, such mergers can be interpreted as pro-competitive, raising goods quantities while lowering prices. The following discussion considers three such modeling variations. First, consider the analysis of imperfect substitutes mergers in Sect. 4.3.; the degree c of substitution in that analysis is a positive number in the range $(0, 1)$, with the limit $c \to 1$ representing perfect substitution. Suppose instead that c is negative, in which case the goods are imperfect complements. With c in the range $(-1, 0)$, formulas (4.15)–(4.16) from Sect. 4.3 imply that merging across imperfect complements is pro-competitive, raising quantity and lowering price. For c close to -1, the goods are near-perfect complements, and a merger of profit-maximizing quantity-choosing competitors is pro-competitive.

As a second approach to modeling possible pro-competitive effects of mergers across perfect complement goods, suppose that firms 1 and 2 don't separately try to pick production quantities pre-merger. Instead, suppose that firm 1 first chooses a price P_1 for its good, then firm 2 chooses a quantity Q_2 for its good, so as to maximize its profit $P_2Q_2 - MC_2Q_2$. From the goods bundle demand curve, $P_1 + dP_2 = a - b(Q_2/d)$, and so $P_2 = ((a - (b/d)Q_2 - P_1)/d$, and profit is:

$$\text{profit, firm 2:} \quad \left(\frac{a - \frac{b}{d}Q_2 - P_1}{d}\right) Q_2 - MC_2Q_2. \tag{4.25}$$

Firm 2's profit-maximizing quantity is:

$$Q_2 = \frac{d^2}{2b}\left(\frac{a - P_1}{d} - MC_2\right), \tag{4.26}$$

and since $Q_2 = dQ_1$, the amount of good Q_1 produced and consumed is:

$$Q_1 = \frac{d}{2b}\left(\frac{a - P_1}{d} - MC_2\right). \tag{4.27}$$

With firm 1 setting the price P_1 for good 1, after which the second firm chooses its quantity Q_2 to maximize its profits, the first firm's profit is $P_1Q_1 - MC_1Q_1$, which after some rearrangement and evaluation of Q_1 takes the form:

$$\text{profit, firm 1:} \quad (P_1 - MC_1)\left(\frac{d}{2b}\left(\frac{a - P_1}{d} - MC_2\right)\right). \tag{4.28}$$

Maximizing profit over price P_1, the resulting duopolist's price is:

$$P_{d1} = \frac{a + MC_1 - dMC_2}{2}, \tag{4.29}$$

Plugging this price formula into the quantity formulas developed earlier, the duopoly quantities are:

$$Q_{d1} = \frac{1}{4b}(a - (MC_1 + dMC_2)) \tag{4.30}$$

$$Q_{d2} = \frac{d}{4b}(a - (MC_1 + dMC_2)) \tag{4.31}$$

Comparing the pre-merger quantities (4.30)–(4.31) to the post-merger quantities (4.22)–(4.23), post-merger quantities are twice as large as pre-merger quantities, so merging doubles output, a pro-competitive effect. With bundle price related to good 1 quantity via $P = a - bQ_1$, a doubling of quantity post-merger causes bundle price to fall by $-bQ_1$ to post-merger P_r from pre-merger P_d:

$$P_d = \frac{1}{4}(3a + MC_1 + dMC_2)$$

While individual market prices are undetermined post-merger, pre-merger price (4.29) for good 1 played a role earlier, and it's worth stating the good 2 price. Given firm 1's choice of P_1, and firm 2's choice of Q_2, and that fact that $P_1 + dP_2 = a - bQ = a - bQ_1$, the price of good 2 is $P_2 = (a - bQ_1 - P_1)/d$ and, plugging in known formulas for P_1 and Q_1, the result is:

$$P_{d2} = \frac{1}{4d}(a - MC_1 + 3dMC_2) \tag{4.32}$$

As a third and final attempt to describe perfect complement mergers as pro-competitive, consider the approach of Cournot (1838) in which each firm chooses its price, conditional on the price choice of the other firm, pre-merger. Firm 1's profit is $(P_1 - MC_1)Q_1$ and since $Q_1 = (P_1 + dP_2 - a)/b$ from the goods bundle demand curve, firm 1's profit is $(P_1 - MC_1)(P_1 + dP_2 - a)/b$, and similarly firm 2's profit is $(P_2 - MC_2)(P_1 + dP_2 - a)/(bd)$. Differentiating firm i's profit with respect to P_i, and setting it equal to 0, for $i = 1, 2$ yields first-order conditions:

$$2P_1 + dP_2 = a + MC_1 \tag{4.33}$$

$$2dP_2 + P_1 = a + dMC_2 \tag{4.34}$$

with solution:

$$P_{d1} = \frac{a + 2MC_1 - dMC_2}{3} \tag{4.35}$$

$$P_{d2} = \frac{a + 2dMC_2 - MC_1}{3d} \tag{4.36}$$

The pre-merger goods bundle's price, $P = P_1 + dP_2$, is then:

$$P_d = \frac{2a + MC_1 + dMC_2}{3} \tag{4.37}$$

which is higher than the post-merger price (4.24). Correspondingly, pre-merger quantities are lower, and given by:

$$Q_{d1} = \frac{1}{3b} (a - (MC_1 + dMC_2)) \tag{4.38}$$

$$Q_{d2} = \frac{d}{3b} (a - (MC_1 + dMC_2)) \tag{4.39}$$

4.4.2 Imperfect Complements

As discussed in Sect. 4.4.1, a repurposing of formulas (4.15)–(4.16) from Sect. 4.3 yields the conclusion that a merger across imperfect complement markets is pro-competitive, raising output and lowering price, under the simplifying assumptions of Sect. 4.3. The remainder of this section illustrates this point via a specific example.

Example 4.5 For goods 1 and 2, let the demand curves be:

good 1 demand curve: $P_1 = 10 - Q_1 - \frac{1}{2}P_2$,

good 2 demand curve: $P_2 = 10 - Q_2 - \frac{1}{2}P_1$,

Using the demand curves to express prices on the left and quantities on the right:

$P_1 = \frac{20}{3} - \frac{4}{3}Q_1 + \frac{2}{3}Q_2$,

$P_2 = \frac{20}{3} + \frac{2}{3}Q_1 - \frac{4}{3}Q_2$.

Pre-merger, the ith firm's profit is:

$$\text{profit}_1 = \left(\frac{20}{3} - \frac{4}{3}Q_1 + \frac{2}{3}Q_2\right)Q_1 - MCQ_1$$

$$\text{profit}_2 = \left(\frac{20}{3} - \frac{4}{3}Q_2 + \frac{2}{3}Q_1\right)Q_2 - MCQ_2.$$

Firm i maximizes profit at that quantity Q_i at which marginal profit equals 0, and the implied conditions on quantities are:

$$\frac{20}{3} - \frac{8}{3}Q_1 + \frac{2}{3}Q_2 - MC = 0$$

$$\frac{20}{3} - \frac{8}{3}Q_2 + \frac{2}{3}Q_1 - MC = 0$$

in which case[18]:

$$Q_1 = Q_2 = \frac{10}{3} - \frac{1}{2}MC,$$

and

$$P_1 = P_2 = \frac{40}{9} + \frac{1}{3}MC.$$

The merged firm chooses Q_1 and Q_2 to maximize profit $P_1Q_1 + P_2Q_2 - (MCQ_1 + MCQ_2)$, with prices P_1 and P_2 determined by demand, in which case:

$$\text{profit} = \left(\frac{20}{3} - \frac{4}{3}Q_1 + \frac{2}{3}Q_2\right)Q_1 + \left(\frac{20}{3} - \frac{4}{3}Q_2 + \frac{2}{3}Q_1\right)Q_2 - (MC(Q_1+Q_2))$$

Maximize profit by taking derivative with respect to Q_1 and Q_2, and setting each derivative to zero:

$$\frac{20}{3} - \frac{8}{3}Q_1 + \frac{4}{3}Q_2 - MC = 0$$

$$\frac{20}{3} - \frac{8}{3}Q_2 + \frac{4}{3}Q_1 - MC = 0$$

The solution is[19]:

$$Q_1 = Q_2 = \frac{5}{3} - \frac{1}{4}MC,$$

and:

$$P_1 = P_2 = \frac{50}{9} + \frac{1}{6}MC.$$

The following table shows pre-merger and post-merger equilibrium quantity and price, and the merger effect "post-pre," in each market:

Merger Pre or post?	Quantity	Price
Pre	$(10/3) - (1/2)MC$	$(40/9) + (1/3)MC$
Post	$(5/3) - (1/4)MC$	$(50/9) + (1/6)MC$
Post-pre	$-(5/3) + (1/4)MC$	$(10/9) - (1/6)MC$

With MC in the range $(0, \frac{20}{3})$ that supports positive equilibrium quantities in each market, the difference of "post-pre" in output is negative, meaning that there is less output post-merger. For price, "post-pre" is positive, and price is higher post-merger.

4.5 VERTICAL MERGERS

A vertical merger, whereby an input good's market is merged with that of a good that requires the input, involves goods which go together in order to be of use or utility. Goods that go together have markets in which the demand in one market responds negatively to a price hike in the other. Section 4.4 discussed this negative effect, of cross-market price on demand, in the context of complement goods. Complement goods, like hot dogs and buns, are a different pairing than vertically linked goods like hogs and sausages. Nevertheless, in terms of basic market demand, they can be modeled similarly.

Rephrasing the discussion in Sect. 4.4, for goods having a positive demand relationship—and negative relationship between demand and cross-market price—mergers of individually monopolized markets are pro-competitive under simplifying assumptions. Applying this reasoning to vertically related goods, mergers of individually monopolized vertically linked markets are pro-competitive, raising output and lowering price, under simplifying assumptions. Unlike horizontal mergers, no efficiencies or synergies in joint production are required for vertical mergers to be pro-competitive.[20]

To model vertical mergers in very simple terms, as earlier let there be two goods, good 1 and good 2, with firm 1 the single producer of good 1 and firm 2 the single producer of good 2. Suppose that the goods are vertically linked, with good 2 a final, consumer good and good 1 an intermediate good used in the production of good 2. Let consumer demand for good 2 have a linear demand curve:

$$P_2 = a - bQ_2, \tag{4.40}$$

with a and b positive parameters, for all Q_2 in the range $(0, a/b)$. Suppose that firm 2 has marginal cost MC_2 of producing each individual unit of good 2, with $a > MC_2$, and that the marginal cost consists of the price P_1, of input or intermediate good 1, plus a wage or other factor cost W.[21] Let firm 1 produce any given unit of good 1 with marginal cost MC_1, and suppose that neither firm 1 nor firm 2 has a fixed cost of operation.

To model the strategic interaction between firms 1 and 2, pre-merger, suppose that firm 1 picks a price for the input good, then firm 2 takes that price and determines its profit-maximizing quantity. Foreseeing the actions of firm 2, firm 1 chooses its price to maximize its own profit.[22] Facing a given price P_1 for good 1, firm 2's profit is $P_2Q_2 - MC_2Q_2$, with $MC_2 = P_1 + W$ and $P_2 = a - bQ_2$. Marginal revenue is $MR_1 = a - 2bQ_2$, which equals marginal cost $P_1 + W$ at the profit-maximizing pre-merger (successive monopoly, or duopoly) quantity choice Q_{d1}, with associated price $P_{d1} = a - bQ_{d1}$:

$$Q_{d2} = \frac{a - (P_1 + W)}{2b} \tag{4.41}$$

$$P_{d2} = \frac{a + (P_1 + W)}{2}. \tag{4.42}$$

Firm 1, knowing firm 2's strategy, picks P_1 to maximize its profits $P_1Q_1 - MC_1Q_1$. By assumption, each unit of good 2 requires 1 unit of good 1, so $Q_1 = Q_2 = Q_{d2}$ is the derived demand for good 1. Firm 2's profit is

$(P_1 - MC_1)Q_{d2} = (P_1 - MC_1)((a - (P_1 + W))/(2b))$. Differentiating profit with respect to P_1, and setting the derivative equal to zero,[23] yields the profit-maximizing price P_{1r}:

$$P_{d1} = \frac{a - W + MC_1}{2}.$$ (4.43)

With quantity $Q_1 = Q_2 = Q_{2d}$, plugging the price formula (4.43) in the quantity formula (4.41), and simplifying, yields optimal pre-merger quantity Q_{d1} for firm 1 and also for firm 2:

$$Q_{d1} = Q_{d2} = \frac{a - (W + MC_1)}{4b}.$$ (4.44)

With good 2's price $P_2 = a - bQ_2$, applying quantity formula (4.44) yields:

$$P_{d2} = \frac{3a + W + MC_1}{4}.$$ (4.45)

Post-merger, the firm sells good 2 at a price $P_2 = a - bQ_2$ and has marginal cost $MC_2 = MC_1 + W$ for each unit produced. The merged firm's profit is $(P_2 - MC_2)Q_2$. The optimal quantity Q_{r2}, and resulting market price P_{r2}, are:

$$Q_{r2} = \frac{a - (W + MC_1)}{2b}$$ (4.46)

$$P_{r2} = \frac{a + (W + MC_1)}{2}.$$ (4.47)

Comparing formulas (4.46) and (4.44), post-merger quantity of the consumer good—good 2—is twice that of the pre-merger quantity, and post-merger price (4.47) is lower than pre-merger price (4.45). This analysis is very similar to one in Sect. 4.4 on mergers across perfect complement goods: pre-merger, firm 1 picks its market's price, and firm 2 picks its quantity, and post-merger quantity doubles.

The literature on vertical mergers shows that the merging of monopolies across vertically linked markets can be pro-competitive, for reasons akin to why complement goods' market mergers can be pro-competitive.

Pre-merger, each firm's choice has indirect consequences for the other firm. These indirect consequences, or externalities, become internalized post-merger, boosting profit and output while lowering price. The idea that vertical mergers can be pro-competitive is companion to the idea that complement goods mergers can be pro-competitive, which in turn is companion to the idea that substitute goods mergers can be anti-competitive. Each idea can be explicated using the same basic economic modeling framework, with variations suited to the behavior particular to substitutes, complements, and vertical links.

Vertically linked firms that merge get to set the price of the downstream good, subject to market demand, but also have a new choice that didn't exist pre-merger, namely, to determine who may buy the upstream good post-merger. If, as assumed earlier, there is a single firm making the upstream good and a single firm making the downstream good, with no other firms or markets in the picture, the merger ends all sales of the upstream good. That good still gets produced but inside the merged firm. After the merger, nobody may buy good 1, but the only other people in the picture are consumers—who are assumed to be interested only in the downstream good. The "foreclosure" of the upstream market post-merger has no impact on consumers.

If the pre-merger market situation is not successive monopoly, as assumed earlier, but instead has multiple firms upstream and/or downstream, the merger's foreclosure of the market for firm 1's product will generally have some consequences for other firms. The assertion that such consequences are anti-competitive is sometimes called the Foreclosure Doctrine. Research, in the 1950s through the 1970s, showed that the anti-competitive effects asserted by Foreclosure Doctrine to be inconsistent with the predictions of simple economic models. This research, associated with a group of scholars whose ideas are referred to as the Chicago School of antitrust economic thought, had a big impact on antitrust law. By the 1980s, vertical mergers were no longer seen as anti-competitive per se. In addition to questioning the anti-competitive effects of foreclosure, the Chicago School also questioned the merit of protecting competitors in vertically linked markets, rather than protecting competition. Today, US antitrust law seems to support the idea of protecting competition, not competitors, with the goal of maximizing consumer surplus.

A second wave of economic research on the foreclosure effects of vertical mergers has shown that these effects can be anti-competitive, with lower quantity and higher price for consumers, depending on who gets foreclosed. The modeling situation gets complicated once multiple upstream and downstream firms are introduced, and an in-depth discussion of foreclosure effects is beyond the scope of this book. Still, it's possible to define a sort of foreclosure effect in a minimalist sort of vertical merger model, as follows. Suppose that there is an "upstream" firm that produces an input or component good, call it good 1, and a "downstream" firm that produces a second component good, call it good 2. The downstream firm also puts the two inputs together as a finished good, with no cost of combining them. The finished good is a bundle consisting of good 1 and good 2. Suppose that each unit of good 1, the "upstream" good, goes together with d units of good 2, the "downstream" good, prior to packaging by the downstream firm. The finished product is bought by consumers, and they too can buy component goods 1 and 2 directly, if they wish, and costlessly bundle them into the finished good. With component goods 1 and 2 having prices P_1 and P_2, respectively, and with each finished good including 1 unit of good 1 and d units of good 2, the price of the finished good is $P = P_1 + dP_2$. Let the consumer demand for the finished good be linear: $P = a - bQ$, with Q the number of units of finished good. As each unit of finished good requires 1 unit of good 1, the quantity Q_1 of good 1 is related to finished goods quantity via $Q_1 = Q$, and for good 2 the corresponding relation is $Q_2 = Q/d$. On the cost side, let each unit of good i have marginal cost MC_i, for $i = 1, 2$.

The vertically linked market model just described is formally the same as the perfect complements model described at the start of Sect. 4.4. As such, a formal conclusion from Sect. 4.4 carries over here: mergers of individually monopolized industries are pro-competitive, under simplifying assumptions. This model is too crude to allow discussion of the foreclosure of competing firms. Even so, the merging firms here do have some foreclosure power, namely, they can close the markets for component goods 1 and 2 to consumers, if desired, making the consumers buy only the bundled good. Would this be a profit-enhancing foreclosure, or a profit-harming one? Since the markets for inputs 1 and 2 both vanish post-merger, so too do their prices P_1 and P_2, leaving the goods bundle price formula $P = P_1 + dP_2$ with little identifiable content post-merger. Maybe foreclosure will harm consumers, but reaching that conclusion from the economic model requires more assumptions. This minimalist exercise in "foreclosure" modeling echoes a theme in the literature on vertical mergers, which is that consumer effects of a merger's foreclosure are highly dependent on the assumptions of the particular model in question.[24]

4.6   PROBLEMS

1. (Independent goods) In the markets for red bell peppers and yellow bell peppers, call red (bell) peppers the first good and yellow peppers the second good. Suppose that red and bell peppers are neither substitutes nor complements, with demand for each being independent of the other's price. Let the demand curves be $P_1 = 20 - Q_1$ and $P_2 = 20 - Q_2$, for the two goods, and let each good be produced at marginal cost $MC = 16$, the same for each unit produced. Let fixed cost be $F = 2$.
   (a) If one firm produces red peppers, and a second one produces yellow peppers, each a monopoly and maximizing profit in their industry, find the equilibrium quantity and price of peppers in each market, and find each firm's profit.
   (b) Suppose now that the two firms merge and, together, maximize profits via the merged firm's choice of quantities. What are the equilibrium quantities, prices, and merged-firm profit?
   (c) Are consumers worse off if firms merge here? Why or why not?
2. (Independent goods, Cobb-Douglas utility) Consider an economy with two goods, such that a representative consumer buys quantities Q_1 and Q_2 of the goods at their respective market prices P_1 and P_2, using income I. Their budget constraint is then $P_1 Q_1 + P_2 Q_2 \le I$. Suppose they choose consumption quantities so as to maximize utility $u(C_1, C_2)$, and let utility take the Cobb-Douglas functional form: $u(C_1, C_2) = C_1^\theta C_2^{1-\theta}$ with preference parameter θ in the range $(0, 1)$. Their utility-maximizing consumption choices are: $C_1 = \frac{\theta I}{P_1}$, $C_2 = \frac{(1-\theta)I}{P_2}$. Supposing that all consumers have identical preferences and income levels, if there are n consumers in the economy then the market-wide (inverse) demand curves are:

$$P_1 = \frac{\theta n I}{Q_1}$$

$$P_2 = \frac{(1-\theta)nI}{Q_2}$$

Suppose that $\theta = 1/2$, $n = 10$ and $I = 1$, and do the following:

(a) Draw the demand curves, on paper, by plotting quantity-price points at quantities 1, 5, 10, 20, and connecting the points. Do they appear linear? Nonlinear?

(b) If the price P_1 of the first good were to rise, would the demand curve for the second good shift up, shift down, or stay the same? Similarly, if the price P_2 of the second good were to rise, would the demand curve for the first good shift up, shift down, or stay the same?

(c) Based on your answers to part xxx, are the two goods independent?

(d) For a monopolist in the first industry, find their optimal quantity choice Q_1 by maximizing profit $P_1 Q_1 - (F_1 + MC_1 Q_1)$, for given values of fixed cost F_1 and marginal cost MC_1, assuming that F_1 is low enough to make a positive quantity profit-maximizing. Similarly, find the profit-maximizing choice for a monopolist in the second industry.

(e) Suppose that monopolists in industries 1 and 2 decide to merge. Their profit is $P_1 Q_1 + P_2 Q_2 - (F_1 + F_2 + MC_1 Q_1 + MC_2 Q_2)$. Show that this profit is maximized at values Q_1 and Q_2 that coincide with the pre-merger quantities you derived in part xx.

3. (Imperfect substitute goods, CES utility) Consider an economy with two goods, such that a representative consumer buys quantities Q_1 and Q_2 of the goods at their respective market prices P_1 and P_2, using income I. Their budget constraint is then $P_1 Q_1 + P_2 Q_2 \leq I$. Suppose they choose consumption quantities so as to maximize utility $u(C_1, C_2)$, and let utility take the Constant Elasticity of Substitution (CES) functional form: $u(C_1, C_2) = C_1^\theta + C_2^\theta$ with preference parameter θ in the range $(0, 1)$. Their utility-maximizing consumption choices Supposing that all consumers have identical preferences and income levels,

Suppose that $\theta = 1/2$, $n = 10$ and $I = 1$, and do the following:

(a) Draw the demand curves, on paper, by plotting quantity-price points at quantities 1, 5, 10, and 20 and connecting the points. Do they appear linear? Nonlinear?

(b) If the price P_1 of the first good were to rise, would the demand curve for the second good shift up, shift down, or stay the same? Similarly, if the price P_2 of the second good were to rise, would the demand curve for the first good shift up, shift down, or stay the same?

(c) Based on your answers to part xxx, are the two goods independent?

(d) For a monopolist in the first industry, find their optimal quantity choice Q_1 by maximizing profit $P_1Q_1 - (F_1 + MC_1Q_1)$, for given values of fixed cost F_1 and marginal cost MC_1, assuming that F_1 is low enough to make a positive quantity profit-maximizing. Similarly, find the profit-maximizing choice for a monopolist in the second industry.

(e) Suppose that monopolists in industries 1 and 2 decide to merge. Their profit is $P_1Q_1 + P_2Q_2 - (F_1 + F_2 + MC_1Q_1 + MC_2Q_2)$. Show that this profit is maximized at values Q_1 and Q_2 that coincide with the pre-merger quantities you derived in part xx.

4. Let the situation be as in Problem 1, but suppose now that red peppers and yellow peppers are substitutes, with the demand for each depending positively on the price of the other. Let the demand curves be:

$$P_1 = 20 - Q_1 - \tfrac{1}{2}Q_2 \text{ and } P_2 = 20 - Q_2 - \tfrac{1}{2}Q_1.$$

(a) If one firm produces red peppers, and a second one produces yellow peppers, each a quantity-choosing monopolist that maximizes profit in their industry—subject to the quantity choice of the other firm—find the equilibrium quantity and price of peppers in each market, and find each firm's profit.

(b) Suppose now that the two firms merge and, together, maximize profits via the merged firm's choice of quantities. What are the equilibrium quantities, prices, and merged-firm profit?

(c) Are consumers worse off if firms merge here? Why or why not?

5. Let the situation be as in Problem ..1, but suppose now that red peppers and yellow peppers are complements, with the demand for each depending negatively on the price of the other. Let the demand curves be:

$$P_1 = 20 - Q_1 + \tfrac{1}{2}Q_2 \text{ and } P_2 = 20 - Q_2 + \tfrac{1}{2}Q_1.$$

(a) If one firm produces red peppers, and a second one produces yellow peppers, each a quantity-choosing monopolist that maximizes profit in their industry—subject to the quantity choice of the other firm—find the equilibrium quantity and price of peppers in each market, and find each firm's profit.

(b) Suppose now that the two firms merge and, together, maximize profits via the merged firm's choice of quantities. What are the equilibrium quantities, prices, and merged-firm profit?

(c) Are consumers worse off if firms merge here? Why or why not?

6. In the market for sugar, suppose that the market demand curve takes the form of the straight line $P = 10 - 2Q$, with price P on the vertical axis and quantity Q (in millions of pounds) on the horizontal axis. The marginal revenue curve is then a straight line $MR = 10 - 4Q$. Let the marginal cost (MC) of producing a pound of sugar be 20 cents.

(a) Graph the demand curve, marginal revenue curve, and marginal cost curve, all on the same graph as in Fig. 3.1.

(b) Find the competitive equilibrium price and quantity, at which the demand curve and marginal cost curve intersect.

(c) Find the pure monopoly equilibrium quantity, at which the marginal revenue and marginal cost curves intersect, and then find the monopoly price.

(d) Compare the competitive equilibrium and monopoly equilibrium outcomes. What seems better for the consumers? Explain.

(e) Compute consumer surplus, producer surplus, and total surplus, in competitive equilibrium and monopoly equilibrium, similar to Example 3.2 in the text.

7. In the US market for high-performance personal computers, let the market demand curve be the straight line $P = 2000 - Q$. Let the marginal cost (MC) equal 1800 for individual, competing firms, and let it be 600 for a monopoly firm.

(a) Graph the demand curve, marginal revenue curve, and marginal cost curves, all on the same graph as in Fig. 3.2.

(b) Find the competitive equilibrium price and quantity, at which the demand curve and competitive marginal cost curve intersect.

(c) Find the monopoly equilibrium quantity, at which the marginal revenue curve and monopoly marginal cost curve intersect, and then find the monopoly price.

(d) Compare the competitive equilibrium and monopoly equilibrium outcomes. What seems better for the consumers? Explain.

(e) Compute consumer surplus, producer surplus, and total surplus, in competitive equilibrium and monopoly equilibrium, similar to Example 3.3 in the text.

8. In the market for tennis rackets, Competitive fringe...

9. Market foreclosure.

NOTES

1. Horizontally related goods are similar goods that sell in the same market or different regional markets. By contrast, vertically related goods have an input-output relationship, with one good an input to production of another, for discussion.

2. The model, proposed by Cournot (1838), is standard economic textbook material, see, for example, Mas-Collel et al. (1995, Section 12.C), Nicholson (2012, Chapter 19), Varian (1992, Chapter 2), and Kreps (1990, Chapter 10).

3. In perfect competition $P = MC$, in which case $a - bQ = MC$ and $Q = (a-MC)/b$. In monopoly, profit is $(a-bQ)Q-MCQ$, maximized at $a-2bQ = MC$, or $Q = (a - MC)/(2b)$ and price $P = a - bQ = (a + MC)/2$.

4. In Table 4.1, the Cournot merger is a contrast between the second and third rows, while the Bertrand merger is a contrast between the first and third rows.

5. Farrell and Shapiro also provide conditions under which merger efficiencies or "synergies" can make a horizontal merger pro-competitive rather than anti-competitive.

6. See xxx.

7. Taking the derivative of merged profit with respect to Q_1, and setting it equal to zero, yields the optimal choice $Q_1 = (a_1 - MC_1)/(2b_1)$ which is the same as the pre-merger optimal choice. A similar argument applies to Q_2.

8. If one of the perfect substitutes had a higher price than the other, consumers would buy only the second and not the first.

9. Validity of this approach requires the first-order conditions to have an "interior" solution, with positive quantity solutions.

10. As earlier, the use of such first-order conditions requires them to have an "interior" solution—nonnegative maximizing quantities.

11. In other words, with no goods substitution, there are no merger effects on quantity, or on price either, consistent with the discussion in Sect. 4.2.

12. The pre-merger maximizing quantities are also the Cournot equilibrium quantities for monopolistic competition. The post-merger profit-maximizing quantities, which are the same as the quantities that result from choosing prices (rather than quantities) to maximize merged-firm profit, appear in Hausman et al. (2011).

13. Note that and $P_1 = 20 - (4/3)Q_1 - (2/3)Q_2 = 20 - (6/3)(6 - (3/10)MC) = 8 + (3/5)MC$, and similarly $P_2 = 8 + (3/5)MC$.

14. As MC is assumed to be a number in the range $(0, 20)$, quantities Q_1 and Q_2 are positive.

15. Prices are then $P_1 = P_2 = 20 - (4/3)Q_1 - (2/3)Q_2 = 20 - (6/3)(5 - (1/4)MC) = 10 + (1/2)MC$.

16. As in the case with no merger, with a merger quantities Q_1 and Q_2 are positive since $MC < a = 10$.

17. .... merger's unilateral effects.

18. Note: $P_1 = P_2 = (20/3) - (4/3)Q_1 + (2/3)Q_2 = (40/9) + (1/3)MC$.

19. Note that quantities are again positive under the assumption that MC lies in $(0, \frac{20}{3})$, and that $P_1 = P_2 = (20/3) - (4/3)Q_1 + (2/3)Q_2 = \frac{50}{9} + \frac{1}{6}MC$.

20. The pro-competitive nature of vertical mergers relies on the assumption that pre-merger markets are individually monopolized. If instead markets are in perfect competition pre-merger, then a merger of any one upstream firm and any one downstream firm results in the same competitive outcome.

21. Assume that one unit of good 1 and one unit of "labor" are used in producing one unit of good 2.

22. The choice variable, for each firm, can be important for equilibrium outcomes in market models, as discussed in Sect. 4.4.

23. Profit is $1/(2b)$ times the expression $(P_1 - MC_1)(a - (P_1 + W))$, and the profit-maximizing P_1 also maximizes the latter expression—whose derivative with respect to P_1 is $-2P + a - W + MC_1$, which equals 0 at $P_1 = (a - W + MC_1)/2$.

24. For further reading on the economic theory of mergers see Buccirossi (2008); Davis and Garcés (2009); Farrell and Shapiro (2010a,a); Faulkner et al. (2012); Hay and Werden (1993); Shapiro (1989); Stigler (1964); and Williamson (1968).

REFERENCES

Buccirossi, P. (2008). *Handbook of antitrust economics.* Cambridge: MIT Press.

Cournot, A. (1838). *Researches into the Mathematical Principles of the Theory of Wealth.* Translated by Nathaniel T. Bacon, with a Bibliography of Mathematical Economics by Irving Fisher, and published by The Macmillan Company (1897, New York, NY).

Davis, P., & Garcés, E. *Quantitative techniques for competition and antitrust analysis.* Princeton: Princeton University Press.

Farrell, J., & Shapiro, C. (1990). Horizontal mergers: An equilibrium analysis. *American Economic Review, 80,* 107–126.

Farrell, J., & Shapiro C. (2010a). Antitrust evaluation of horizontal mergers: An economic alternative to market definition. *The B.E. Journal of Theoretical Economics, 10,* 9.

Farrell J., & Shapiro C. (2010b). Upward pricing pressure and critical loss analysis: Response. *CPI Antitrust Journal,* 1–17.

Faulkner, D., Teerikangas, S., & Joseph, R. J. (2012). *The handbook of mergers and acquisitions*. Oxford: Oxford University Press.

Hausman J, Moresi, S., & Rainey, M. (2011). Unilateral effects of mergers with general linear demand. *Economic Letters, 111*, 119–121.

Hay, G. A., & Werden, G. J. (1993). Horizontal mergers: Law, policy, and economics. *American Economic Review, 83*(2), 173–177; Papers and proceedings of the one hundred and fifth meeting of the American Economic Association (May 1993), pp. 173–177.

Kreps, D. M. (1990). *A course in microeconomic theory*. Princeton: Princeton University Press.

Mas-Collel, A., Whinston, M. D., & Green, J. R. (1995). *Microeconomics theory*. Oxford, UK: Oxford University Press.

Nicholson, W., & Snyder, C. M. (2012). Microeconomic theory: Basic principles and extensions (11th ed.). New York, NY: Cengage Learning.

Shapiro, C. (1989). Theories of oligopoly behavior. In R. Schmalensee & R. D. Willig (Eds.), *Handbook of industrial organization* (Vol. I, pp. 329–414). Amsterdam: North-Holland.

Stigler, G. J. (1964). A theory of oligopoly. *Journal of Political Economy, 72*, 44–61.

Varian, H. R. (1992). *Microeconomic analysis* (3rd ed.). New York: W.W. Norton and Company.

Williamson, O. (1968). Economies as an antitrust defense: The welfare tradeoffs. *American Economic Review, 58*, 18–36.

PART III

Antitrust and Allied Economic Fields

CHAPTER 5

International Trade

Abstract Competition, and market concentration, are key themes in antitrust economics. A lack of competition, or excess of concentration, can have anti-competitive effects, lowering the amount of goods available to consumers while raising prices. In the case of mergers, a merger of pure duopoly firms into a single firm is anti-competitive, under the assumptions maintained in Chap. 4, as is a merger of monopolies in industries that produce goods which consumers regard as substitutes. But a merger of monopolies in industries producing complement goods, or vertically linked goods, can be pro-competitive, raising output and lowering price. Sometimes, an increase in market concentration benefits consumers.

The idea that greater market concentration can increase consumer surplus is a very old one, predating the modern antitrust era. In particular, the theory of international trade—pioneered by Adam Smith, David Ricardo, and others in the 1700s and 1800s—dwells on the process of specialization and exchange, whereby each nation or producer creates that good in which it has a comparative advantage, leaving to others the production of other goods. The rationale is efficiency: improved efficiency with specialization can yield greater output and consumer welfare for society as a whole. In Chap. 2's discussion of pure monopoly, efficiencies afforded by the combining of firms made possible greater consumer welfare. In trade theory, efficiencies play a similar role.

© The Author(s) 2018
S. Gilbert, *Multi-Market Antitrust Economics*, Quantitative
Perspectives on Behavioral Economics and Finance,
https://doi.org/10.1007/978-3-319-69386-6_5

This chapter covers some basic theory of international trade, with an eye toward its logical connection to monopoly and antitrust issues. Themes of equity and fairness appear that are relevant for trade and antitrust, and some cross-fertilization of each field may benefit both. As in previous chapters, ideas are supported using graphs and simple models analyzed in some detail. Also, the multi-market theme of the book carries over here, with inclusion of goods trade and also resource markets.

Keywords Production   possibilities   •   Efficiency   •   Fairness • Specialization • Coordinated production • Comparative advantage

5.1   ONE-PERSON ECONOMY

As a starting point, consider a world inhabited by just one person. Economic textbooks cast such a world in terms of the Robinson Crusoe story, with shipwrecked Crusoe alone on an island.[1] Suppose that Crusoe can devote up to eight hours per day working and that the only productive work is the gathering and harvesting of coconuts—the only food source, with Crusoe able to gather and harvest one coconut per hour.

In this one-person economy, there is only one industry—the coconut industry—and for that industry there is only one factor of production, labor. Crusoe provides all the labor and acts as the only firm in the coconut industry. His firm, call it Crusoe's Coconuts, is a monopoly. His only customer is himself, and he consumes all the coconuts. Crusoe's Coconuts is a "good" monopoly by the standards set forth earlier:

- It's efficient in production terms, provided that the factors of production are put to full use—which they are if Crusoe works eight hours per day.
- It's fair in terms of the distribution of goods: Crusoe provides all the factors of production, and he receives all the goods produced.
- It's efficient in terms of consumption opportunities: Crusoe consumes as much as he is able to produce.

The Crusoe one-person economy is a story with specific economic assumptions, and so forms an economic model. It's a very simple model, but in economics and other sciences, models should be kept as simple as possible, for the purposes of the intended analysis. In the one-person economic model, monopoly is good in terms that are easily checked. Also, while the model makes specific assumptions about the coconut industry: eight hours of labor available, one coconut collected and harvested per hour, the conclusions about monopoly would be the same if instead ten hours of labor were available, two coconuts were processed per hour, and so on. In other words, the numbers in the model provide a concrete illustration of monopoly, but the conclusions are valid more generally.

5.2   TWO-GOOD, TWO-PERSON ECONOMY

Consider now an island inhabited by two people: castaway Crusoe and island native Friday. Friday is able to gather and harvest coconuts, one coconut per hour, and is able to fish—catching two fish per hour. Crusoe is able to harvest two coconut per hour and is able to catch one fish per hour. Suppose that both Crusoe and Friday can work up to eight hours per day.

In this island economy there are two goods—coconuts and fish—and two people. There may be a monopoly in the supply of either coconuts or fish, if only one person provides them, or there may be no monopoly in either industry. Unlike the one-person economic model described earlier, with two people and two goods, it's not obvious whether monopoly is good, bad, or neither.

One way that monopoly could occur is if Crusoe and Friday decided to live separately on two halves of the island, Crusoeland and Fridayland. Working separately and consuming only their own coconuts and fish, each would be monopolists in their own society. With no economic transactions or trade among Crusoeland and Fridayland, economists would call the result autarky. Monopoly in this autarky situation is not all good, nor all bad, using the three criteria discussed earlier:

- Monopoly is inefficient in production terms, even if factors of production are put to full use—with Crusoe and Friday working eight hours per day. The inefficiency comes from the failure of Crusoe and Friday to coordinate their production efforts. That's a sign of a bad monopoly.

- Monopoly is fair in terms of the distribution of goods: Crusoe and Friday each provide all the factors of production in their respective lands, and each receives all the goods produced.
- Monopoly is inefficient in terms of consumption opportunities, due to the failure to coordinate production and create more consumable goods.

Another way that monopoly could occur is if Crusoe and Friday coordinate their production efforts, with either Crusoe or Friday specializing by working in only one industry, and then exchange some fish harvested by one of them for some coconuts harvested by the other. In particular, suppose that Crusoe specializes in producing coconuts, harvesting two per hour, and 16 total each day, while Friday specializes in fishing, likewise harvesting 16 total. Suppose Crusoe exchanges eight coconuts for eight of Friday's fish daily, in which case each person gets eight coconuts and eight fish.

With coordinated production and exchange of coconuts for fish, Crusoe gets eight coconuts and eight fish, whereas in autarky he could have eight coconuts but only four fish with them, and with eight fish he could have no coconuts. Friday's outcome, with coordination, is advantageous in terms analogous to those for Crusoe. This monopoly is mostly good, maybe all good, in the following terms:

- With coordinated production, efficiency can be no less than without coordination, provided that the coordination is aimed at making production as efficient as possible. If efficient coordination leads to monopoly, that's good in terms of production and efficiency. The coordinated exchange outcome with 16 fish and 16 coconuts produced daily on the island is efficient in the sense that, with the number of coconuts set at 16 the most fish that Crusoe and Friday could get is 16, and likewise with the number of fish set at 16 the most coconuts they could get is 16.
- The distribution of goods, to Crusoe and Friday, is fair in that each works the same amount of time and ends up with the same amount of goods. Also, while hours worked are not a complete description of labor as a factor of production, Crusoe and Friday are similar in terms of productivity per hour, though different in terms of the industries in

which they work best, so neither is more "deserving" of goods than the other. In terms of fairness, this monopoly outcome is good.

- The economy is at least partly efficient in terms of consumption opportunities: production efficiency makes available an abundance of goods, and exchange makes these available to consumers. However, the result is that each person consumes an equal amount of coconuts and fish, whereas consumer preferences may lean toward a greater share of one good than the other, in which case a different production plan may lead to improved consumer happiness.

Compared to the one-person economic model, the two-person model is more complex, making it somewhat harder to say whether a given monopoly situation is good or not. One of these complexities is that there are two sorts of outcomes in the two-person model: autarky and exchange. Also, the productivity numbers—coconuts and fish harvested per hour—for Crusoe and Friday are not purely illustrative: the substantive conclusions about monopoly can be quite different depending on what these numbers are.

While the Crusoe-Friday economy is just one example of how coordination, monopoly, and exchange can be good, the principle is more general. Since coordination of production plans is voluntary and mutually beneficial when the plan is to maximize efficiency, coordination is good or, at least, not bad. Too, coordination involves putting resources—or factors of production—to their best and most efficient use, and this will involve some specialization if some person's resources are best used in one industry, while another's are best used in another industry. The result might be monopoly in each industry, as in the above example, or a less extreme form of specialization.

Coordination and specialization are generally good, in terms of production efficiency, but it's not obvious whether they generally result in a fair distribution of goods to households. In the example earlier, Crusoe gathers 16 coconuts, Friday catches 16 fish, and each trades half their catch with the other. Each is a monopolist and ends up with eight coconuts and eight fish, and each puts in the same amount of labor—eight hours. This is fair, but other examples—with different patterns of productivity for Crusoe and Friday—might end up with one person getting more goods than the other: this can still be fair if the person that gets more goods is also more productive in fishing and coconut gathering.

Distribution fairness, with coordination and exchange, unfolds in two segments. The first segment is where households provide factors of production to industry. With just one factor—labor—suppose that each household initially takes home a share of each good they produce, with the share in proportion to the hours they contributed to the production of the good. In this first segment, households receive as "income" a bundle of goods. In the second segment, they exchange goods, thereby spending their income. The first of these segments is fair in distribution terms, and it remains to determine the fairness of exchange.

An exchange of goods, between households in a simplified world with no money, is voluntary and affords equal opportunity for each household to negotiate or haggle. There is no sense in which exchange is unfair, and the presence of this second segment of the production and exchange process does not take away from the distributional fairness of the first segment. On the whole, coordinated production and exchange achieves distributional fairness, even when coordination creates monopoly.

5.3   MONOPOLY AND PRODUCTION EFFICIENCY

Coordinated production, in the two-person two-good economy, can lead to specialization and monopoly, for efficiency's sake, as shown earlier. To state more generally the connection between monopoly and productive efficiency, it's helpful to take a more systematic approach. For economists, "systematic" tends to mean mathematically structured. Readers willing to see some math at work can usefully read through this section, while readers preferring to stick with the conclusions that math provides may wish to skip to the end of this section.

To restate the two-person two-good economy in more systematic terms, suppose there is a single resource—labor—with persons a and b each able to work up to some number $\bar{L}$ of hours per day. Also, let there be two industries, industry 1 and industry 2. Let L_{a1} be the hours worked each day by person a in industry 1, let L_{a2} the hours worked by a in industry 2, and define L_{b1} and L_{b2} analogously.

Constraints on resources, or factors of production, are key to determining production possibilities. For persons a and b, the relevant resource constraint is that they can only work $\bar{L}$ hours per day, a fact stated below as a pair of equations.

Resource Constraints

$$L_{a1} + L_{a2} = \bar{L} \tag{5.1}$$

$$L_{b1} + L_{b2} = \bar{L} \tag{5.2}$$

With a given amount of labor, each person can produce some quantity of goods. Suppose that for each person and each industry an additional unit of labor provides some additional output, and that the amount of additional output is the same for each additional unit of labor provided. With L symbolizing labor, Q symbolizing output quantity, and c symbolizing the additional or marginal output per unit of input, production possibilities appear below as a set of four equations, with output expressed as a function of input.

Production Functions

$$Q_{a1} = m_{a1}L_{a1} \tag{5.3}$$

$$Q_{a2} = m_{a2}L_{a2} \tag{5.4}$$

$$Q_{b1} = m_{b1}L_{b1} \tag{5.5}$$

$$Q_{b2} = m_{b2}L_{b2} \tag{5.6}$$

The first of these equations says that the labor hours L_{a1} provided by a to industry 1 generate a quantity Q_{a1} of good 1 equal to $m_{a1}L_{a1}$ units, with m_{a1} the marginal output or product for person a and good 1. The remaining three equations are similar, covering good 2 and also person b.

To illustrate, recall that in the Crusoe-Friday example, the work day is eight hours long and the amounts of coconuts and fish produced per hour by each person are as follows:

Person	Coconuts	Fish
Crusoe	2	1
Friday	1	2

Applying the above mathematical notation, $\bar{L} = 8$, and letting person a be Crusoe and person b be Friday, the marginal products are $m_{a1} = 2$, $m_{a2} = 1$, $m_{b1} = 1$, and $m_{b2} = 2$.

Marginal products are key to determining the extent to which product coordination begets monopoly in an industry. One way of interpreting patterns in marginal product, across persons a and b, is in terms of absolute advantage. Person a has an absolute advantage in producing good 1, compared to person b, if a's marginal product for good 1 is higher than that of b: $m_{a1} > m_{b1}$. Analogously, a has an absolute advantage in producing good 2 if $m_{a2} > m_{b2}$. In the Crusoe-Friday example, Crusoe has an absolute advantage in coconuts, Friday in fish.

Another important pattern in productivity differences is comparative advantage. Person a has a comparative advantage in producing good 1 if they incur a lower opportunity cost than b does in producing good 1. Opportunity cost here means the amount of good 2 foregone to to produce one more unit of good 1. In terms of marginal products, comparative advantage involves a comparison of two ratios, person a's ratio of marginal products for good 1 and 2, and person b's ratio of marginal products also, as shown below.

Comparative Advantage

$$\frac{m_{a1}}{m_{a2}} > \frac{m_{b1}}{m_{b2}} \tag{5.7}$$

By coordinating production, persons a and b can decide a production plan that makes efficient use of their combined resources. Let Q_1 be the total amount of the first good produced, this being the sum $Q_{a1} + Q_{b1}$ of good 1 produced by a and b, and similarly let Q_2 be the total amount of the second good produced. For any feasible amount Q_1 of the first good, let $Q_2^*(Q_1)$ be the greatest amount of good 2 that a and b can produce via coordinated production. The available production possibilities are determined by the resource constraints—Eqs. (5.1) and (5.2), and the production functions—Eqs. (5.3) through (5.6). Making best use of these possibilities, the efficient quantity $Q_2^*(Q_1)$ of the second good, for each feasible amount Q_1 of the first good, is shown below and labeled the production possibilities frontier, abbreviated PPF below.

Production Possibilities Curve

$$Q_2^*(Q_1) = \begin{cases} m_{b2}\bar{L} - (m_{b_2}/m_{b1})Q_1 \text{ if } Q_1 \leq m_{a1}\bar{L} \\ (m_{a2} + m_{b2})\bar{L} - (m_{b_2}/m_{b1})Q_1 \text{ if } m_{a1}\bar{L} \leq Q_1 \leq (m_{a1} + m_{b1})\bar{L} \end{cases}$$
$$(5.8)$$

This somewhat complicated formula describes a curve—the PPF curve—in the sense that the function $Q_2^*(Q_1)$ can be graphed or plotted as a curve on a chalkboard or piece of paper, with Q_1 on the horizontal axis and $Q_2^*(Q_1)$ on the vertical axis. In the Crusoe-Friday example, the PPF curve is as follows:

$$Q_2^*(Q_1) = \begin{cases} 24 - Q_1/2 \text{ if } Q_1 \leq 16 \\ 32 - Q_1 \text{ if } 16 \leq Q_1 \leq 32 \end{cases}$$
$$(5.9)$$

The following graph shows the Crusoe-Friday PPF curve.
At point A in Fig. 5.1, Crusoe is a monopolist in coconuts—providing 16 of them—and Friday is a monopolist in fish, also providing 16. The PPF

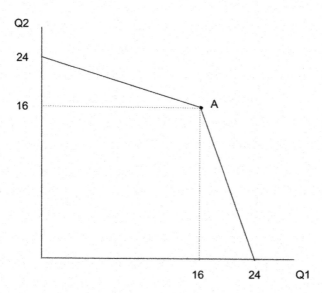

Fig. 5.1 Production possibility frontier

curve consists of the point A together with two solid line segments: the one extending left and up to the value 24 on the vertical axis, and the one extending down and right toward the value 24 on the horizontal axis. At points on the PPF to the left of A, Crusoe is a monopolist in coconuts but both Crusoe and Friday supply fish, whereas at points on the PPF to the right of A, Friday is a monopolist in fish but both Crusoe and Friday supply coconuts.

In the Crusoe-Friday economy, coordinated production always creates a monopoly, in one or both goods. The same is true with the more general sort of production possibilities defined by Eqs. (5.1)–(5.6). When Q_1 equals $m_{a1}\bar{L}$, coordinated production creates a monopoly in both goods, with person a specializing in the first good and person b specializing in the second good. When Q_1 is less than $m_{a1}\bar{L}$, person a holds a monopoly in good 1, but both a and b produce good 2. When Q_1 is greater than $m_{a1}\bar{L}$ then person b holds a monopoly in good 2, but both a and b produce good 1.

When one person has a comparative advantage over another, in the production of a good, coordinated production is only efficient if there is a monopoly in at least one good. If instead no one has a comparative advantage over the other, monopoly in some good or industry is not necessary for productive efficiency, but monopoly still achieves efficiency. To see why, suppose as earlier that the world consists of two people—a and b—but now suppose that neither has a comparative advantage in good 1 or good 2. In terms of marginal products, a lack of comparative advantage means that the ratio of marginal products for goods 1 and 2 is the same for persons a and b:

$$\frac{m_{a1}}{m_{a2}} = \frac{m_{b1}}{m_{b2}} \tag{5.10}$$

In this context, the production possibilities frontier is a straight line, having the same slope at all values of the first good's quantity Q_1. By contrast, when one person has a comparative advantage, the PPF is not a straight line but instead is composed of two straight lines joined together. The PPF straightens out when there is no comparative advantage, and for the readers familiar with algebra of straight lines, this can be gleaned from the PPF formula (5.8) wherein the ratios that determine comparative advantage, or lack thereof,[2] also determine the slope of the PPF.

With no comparative advantage, a monopoly in each industry is still efficient and puts the economy on the straight-line PPF, but while every

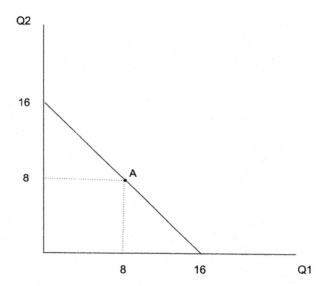

Fig. 5.2 Linear production possibility frontier

situation with a monopoly in one or more industries is on the PPF, so is every situation in which both persons *a* and *b* work full time. With no comparative advantage, the only requirement for efficiency is that both people use all their factors of production. To illustrate, Fig. 5.2 shows the PPF for a variant of the Crusoe-Friday economy in which both Crusoe and Friday get one coconut per hour of work, and likewise get one fish per hour of work. Pure monopoly, with both Crusoe and Friday working only in one industry, is represented by Point A in Fig. 5.2, but this point also represents all non-monopoly situations where Crusoe and Friday put a total of eight hours in industry 1, and a total of eight hours in industry 2. All other full-time work situations are also represented on the straight-line PPF in this graph.

5.4   MONOPOLY AND CONSUMER HAPPINESS

If a monopoly situation achieves production efficiency then it is "good" in an important way, but need not make households as happy as they might be. After production, goods are divvied up by households, and this distribution of goods to households may leave them happy, or not. In a two-person economy with specialization and exchange, the divvying up starts with each producing some goods—their "endowment"—then exchanging goods with the other person. By receiving the product of their labor, each person is receiving a fair share of the goods produced. Also, goods exchange may be fair, and overall each household may feel that goods distribution is fair and equitable.

Monopoly—via specialization and exchange—can make households as happy as they can be in terms of goods received and consumption opportunities provided. The link between monopoly and consumer happiness depends on the terms on which producers exchange goods with each other. Exchange might be based on a simple sharing rule, or the ruling of an arbitrator or hypothetical social planner, or a market transaction. The following passages explore each of these exchange possibilities, all of which illustrate the idea that monopoly can promote consumer happiness.

5.4.1   Goods Distribution via Sharing

In a two-person world with completely specialized production, suppose that person a specializes in good 1 and person b specializes in good 2. At the end of the work day, person a has a bunch of good 1 and none of good 2, while person b has a bunch of good 2 and none of good 1. Put yourself in the shoes of one of these two people, standing around with a pile of goods, wanting to swap some of your goods pile with some from the other pile. Would it not be reasonable to exchange half your pile for half of the other person's pile?

In the Crusoe-Friday economy in Sect. 5.2, if Crusoe is a monopolist in coconuts and Friday is a monopolist in fish, they can share half their product with each other, each consuming eight coconuts and eight fish per day. This is a simple way to distribute goods to households, and this monopoly outcome may makes both Crusoe and Friday as happy as possible—in terms of goods consumption. To see why, consider their choices in autarky—without coordinated production and monopoly. Table 5.1 shows the production possibilities for each person in autarky—each person on their own.

Neither Crusoe nor Friday can get eight units each of coconuts and fish in autarky. Crusoe can get eight coconuts, but only with four fish, while Friday can get eight fish but only with four coconuts. If each person

Table 5.1   Production possibilities in autarky

Crusoe		Friday	
Coconuts	Fish	Coconuts	Fish
0	8	0	16
2	7	1	14
4	6	2	12
6	5	3	10
8	4	4	8
10	3	5	6
12	2	6	4
14	1	7	2
16	0	8	0

likes each good about the same, coordinated production and monopoly exchange can make each person happier than they would be as autarky monopolists—providing only for themselves. If instead somebody likes one of the goods much more than the other, then they may prefer autarky over coordination and exchange. For example, if Crusoe really likes coconuts but doesn't like fish much, then he may prefer autarky with ten coconuts and three fish, rather than specialization and exchange with eight coconuts and eight fish.[3]

Consumer preferences partly determine whether specialization and monopoly can make consumers happy. Another determinant is the extent of production advantages of one person over another. In the Crusoe-Friday economy, Crusoe has an absolute and comparative advantage in coconuts, while Friday has an absolute and comparative advantage in fish. This symmetry is ideal for specialization and exchange. If instead one person has an absolute advantage in both goods then they may be better off without specialization and exchange.

Example 5.4.1 In the Crusoe-Friday economy, suppose now that Friday is super-productive, able to produce ten coconuts per hour, or alternatively 20 fish per hour, and she dominates Crusoe with an absolute advantage in the production of each good, as shown in Table 5.2.

If Crusoe and Friday completely specialize their production according to their comparative advantages, and then exchange goods via equal-split sharing, each ends up with eight coconuts and 80 fish. In autarky, Crusoe

Table 5.2 Marginal products with one dominant producer

Person	Coconuts	Fish
Crusoe	2	1
Friday	10	20

can produce eight coconuts but only four fish, and may or may not prefer exchange to autarky, depending on how much he likes fish. On the other hand, Friday can produce 40 coconuts and 80 fish in autarky,[4] and this is way better than the eight coconuts + 80 fish she would get via exchange.

Monopoly can make consumers happy, and in a two-person economy, this connection is clearest when there is some symmetry in preference among goods and in absolute advantage among producers. To explore this connection further, suppose that happiness depends only on how much each household in the economy gets to consume of each good. To be systematic in accounting for consumer happiness, economists model or represent it using utility functions. With the quantities of goods consumed being an input to the utility function, the output is a number or score that represents the person's satisfaction or happiness associated with the consumption bundle. Suppose also that the utility number goes up when amounts of goods consumption rise, and goes down when consumption falls.

With a utility interpretation of household happiness, consider again the two-person two-good economy of Sect. 5.2. In that economy, with coordinated production and exchange, monopoly in one or more industries may lead to greatest happiness—meaning that in order to make some household better off, it would be necessary to make some other household worse off—a situation economists call Pareto optimal or Pareto efficient. Other economic outcomes may also be Pareto efficient, including the one where there is no coordinated production and each person acts as monopoly in their own economy. To say that any one economic outcome achieves consumer happiness via Pareto efficiency is to say that outcome does not make all consumers unhappy, a relatively weak form of praise.

To get a firmer grip on utility and Pareto optimality, it's helpful to be more systematic—which as earlier is a code word for math intensive, signaling a fork in the road where readers can plow on or skip to the end of this section. For persons a and b in a two-person economy, let C_{a1} be the amount of good 1 consumed by person a, C_{a2} the amount of good 2 consumed by a, and let C_{b1} and C_{b2} be the corresponding consumption amounts for person 2. Coordinated production yields goods quantities Q_a for person a and Q_b for person b, and for trading purposes these are called the endowments of a and b. With person a trading some of their goods for those of person b, the result of trade is a pair of consumption bundles C_a and C_b, with C_a consisting of C_{a1} and C_{a2}, and C_b consisting of C_{b1} and C_{b2}. Trading occurs at some rate of exchange, or price, for each good. Let p_1 be the exchange price of good 1, and let p_2 be the exchange price of good 2. Assume that both p_1 and p_2 are positive, and without loss of generality let good 1 be numeraire good—for which price p_1 is set equal to 1. Then persons a and b choose a consumption bundle subject to their budget constraints, which depend on prices p and endowments Q, as shown below.

Household Consumption Budgets

$$p_1 C_{a1} + p_2 C_{a2} = p_1 Q_{a1} + p_2 Q_{a2} \tag{5.11}$$

$$p_1 C_{b1} + p_2 C_{b2} = p_1 Q_{b1} + p_2 Q_{b2} \tag{5.12}$$

In addition to household-specific budget constraints, the total amount of consumption of each good must equal the amount of that good produced, as shown below.

Consumption-Endowment Balance

$$C_{a1} + C_{b1} = Q_{a1} + Q_{b1} \tag{5.13}$$

$$C_{a2} + C_{b2} = Q_{a2} + Q_{b2} \tag{5.14}$$

In a two-person economy, if person a produces only good 1 and shares half of it with person b, and person b produces only good 2 and shares half of it with person a, then, applying the idea of production functions—via Eqs. (5.3)–(5.6), the result is: $Q_{a1} = m_{a1}\bar{L}$, $Q_{a2} = 0$, $Q_{b1} = 0$, $Q_{b2} = m_{b2}\bar{L}$, and consumption levels are $C_{a1} = C_{b1} = m_{a1}\bar{L}/2$ for good 1, and $C_{a2} = C_{b2} = m_{b1}\bar{L}/2$ for good 2.

With good 1 the numeraire good, its price p_1 equals 1, and the price p_2 of good 2 (in terms of good 1) is the amount of good 1 exchanged divided by the amount of good 2 exchanged, this being $(Q_{a1}/2)/(Q_{b2}/2)$, in which case p_2 fits the following description:

Price of Second Good, With Sharing

$$p_2 = \frac{Q_1}{Q_2} \tag{5.15}$$

Expressing output quantities Q in terms of productivities, price p_2 also takes the form of a productivity ratio $p_2 = m_{a1}/m_{b2}$.

In the Crusoe-Friday economy of Sect. 5.2, consumption levels are eight each for coconuts and fish, for both Crusoe and Friday, and the price of fish in terms of coconuts is, from Eq. (5.15), $p_2 = 1$. As the reader can check, this outcome satisfies the household budget equations (5.11)–(5.12) and the consumption-endowment balance equations (5.13)–(5.14).

To capture the possibility that people may like one good more than another, or instead have equal preference for each good, economists have a special utility function called the Cobb-Douglas utility function, whose formula appears below.

Cobb-Douglas Utility

$$U(C_1, C_2) = C_1^w C_2^{1-w} \tag{5.16}$$

where w is a number which is greater than 0 and less than 1. For each household, utility applies to their own consumption levels. So, for person a their Cobb-Douglas utility is $C_{a1}^w C_{a2}^{1-w}$, while for person b it is $C_{b1}^w C_{b2}^{1-w}$. A higher value of the number w indicates a greater desire for good 1, relative to good 2.

Returning to the connection between monopoly and consumer happiness, suppose there is symmetry in preference among goods, meaning that the preference rate w for good 1 is the same as the rate $1 - w$, each

Table 5.3 Utility in autarky

Crusoe			Friday		
Coconuts	Fish	Utility	Coconuts	Fish	Utility
0	8	0.0	0	16	0.0
2	7	3.7	1	14	3.7
4	6	4.9	2	12	4.9
6	5	5.5	3	10	5.5
8	4	5.7	4	8	5.7
10	3	5.5	5	6	5.5
12	2	4.9	6	4	4.9
14	1	3.7	7	2	3.7
16	0	0.0	8	0	0.0

rate equal to $1/2$. With this assumption, for the Crusoe-Friday economy of Sect. 5.2 specialization and exchange via sharing produces the greater utility for both Crusoe and Friday than does autarky. With specialization and sharing, each person consumes eight coconuts and eight fish, and their utility value is $u(C_1, C_2) = 8^{1/2} \times 8^{1/2} = 8$. By comparison, utility values are all smaller than eight in autarky, as shown in Table 5.3.

5.4.2 Distribution via Social Planner

Sharing, as a means of splitting up goods after specialization and exchange, may sound too nice for folks whose aim is to achieve high levels of consumption for themselves. As an alternative, suppose that both people in a two-person economy agree to follow a rule determined by some hypothetical, egalitarian referee or arbitrator or social planner. Suppose that the social planner's goal is find the production and exchange plan that maximizes "social welfare"—itself a function of the consumption utility for persons a and b. Given utility functions U_a and U_b for persons a and b, a simple, egalitarian, social welfare function W is the following:

$$W = U_a + U_b \tag{5.17}$$

Social planning can lead to simple sharing of goods produced by monopolists, in which case monopoly can be good—for reasons discussed earlier. To illustrate, in the Crusoe-Friday economy of Sect. 5.2, specialization and simple sharing yields utility values $U_a = U_b = 8$. These utility values are higher than what could be achieved in autarky, for each person, so social welfare—the sum of utility values—is higher with sharing than in autarky.

Simple, or equal, sharing may also beat unequal sharing of goods produced, in terms of social welfare W. For example, equal sharing beats unequal sharing if each person has Cobb-Douglas utility preferences with the same preference rates for each good. On the other hand, if consumers have a stronger preference for one good over another, a social planner may choose unequal sharing, with a price price p_2 of the second good (in terms of the first) which is either greater or less than the equal-sharing value shown earlier in Eq. (5.15).

Monopoly can lead to consumer happiness even if producers do not initially agree to share the fruits of their labor, provided that their ultimate trade is consistent with the wisdom of some hypothetical, benevolent social planner. Consumer preferences, for one good versus the other, can strongly effect the ultimate desirability of monopoly and patterns of trade, as discussed earlier. To take this idea a step further, the next section takes closer look at prices and their effect on utility-maximizing consumer choice and trade.

5.4.3   Distribution via Trade

Suppose that households trade so as to achieve the highest utility, given their endowment and constraints imposed by consumption budgets and the balance of consumption and endowments. Utility is a function of consumption, let $U(C_a)$ be person a's utility function, with C_a the pair of consumption amounts for goods 1 and 2, and let $U(C_b)$ be b's utility function. Let the utility functions U be increasing in consumption amounts C. To get consumption C, a and b coordinate production, creating quantities Q of goods, then they exchange goods and consume the amount of goods they ultimately receive from production and exchange. If utility functions U are increasing in consumption C at a rate that diminishes as C gets bigger then there is diminishing marginal utility. If the functions $U(C)$ are also smooth, having well-defined rates of instantaneous change at each value of C, then there is only one possible value for prices p for which each household maximizes utility subject to their budget constraints (5.11)–(5.12) and subject to the consumption-endowment balance (5.13)–(5.14). These are the Walrasian equilibrium prices, denoted as p^*. In Walrasian equilibrium, for a given set of endowments the outcome for households is Pareto efficient.

In the two-person two-good economy, equilibrium consumption levels are determined by labor choices by both people plus labor productivity and the exchange of goods produced by labor. The Pareto optimal production-exchange outcomes are those that have utility numbers $U(C_a)$ and $U(C_b)$ for persons a and b such that any other production-exchange outcome cannot achieve a higher value of one utility $U(C_a)$ or $U(C_b)$ without incurring a lower value for the other one. Pareto optimal outcomes, in an economy with production and exchange equilibrium, depend on labor hours, labor productivities, and also household utility or preference for goods 1 and 2.

With Cobb-Douglas utility, at given prices p each person maximizes utility by spending a share w of their income on the first good, and a share $1 - w$ on the second good. Income for person a is $p_1 Q_{a1} + p_2 Q_{a2}$, with shorthand Y_1, and income for person b is $p_1 Q_{b1} + p_2 Q_{b2}$ with shorthand Y_2. Consumption levels are then $C_{a1} w Y_1$, $C_{a2} = (1 - w)Y_1$ for person 1, and

Optimal Consumption, Cobb-Douglas Utility

$$C_{a1} = wY_1 \tag{5.18}$$

$$C_{a2} = (1 - w)Y_1 \tag{5.19}$$

$$C_{b1} = wY_2 \tag{5.20}$$

$$C_{b2} = (1 - w)Y_2 \tag{5.21}$$

From the foregoing it follows that the ratio of spending on good 1 and good 2 equals the ratio of preference rates for good 1 and good 2:

$$\frac{p_1 Q_1}{p_2 Q_2} = \frac{w}{1 - w} \tag{5.22}$$

With Cobb-Douglas utility, equilibrium prices p^* depend on the rate of preference w for the first good, plus the total amounts Q_1 and Q_2 of goods 1 and 2 produced. Recalling that good 1 is the numeraire good, its price equals one by definition, and Eq. (5.22) provides a formula for the remaining equilibrium price:

$$p_2^* = \frac{1 - w}{w} \frac{Q1}{Q2} \tag{5.23}$$

If rate w of good 1 preference is the same as the rate $1 - w$ for good 2 preference, then the equilibrium price (5.23) reduces to the equal-sharing price (5.15) shown earlier.

Example 5.4.2 In the Crusoe-Friday economy with productivities as shown in above Table (see Sect. 5.3), let Crusoe and Friday each have consumption preferences of the Cobb-Douglas type, with rates of preference w and $1 - w$ of good 1 and good 2 preference are equal, in which case $w = 1/2$. Crusoe and Friday coordinate production, reaching the production possibility frontier (PPF) in Fig. 5.1, then exchange goods at equilibrium prices so as to consume[5] in a way that maximizes their utility subject to budget and endowment-consumption constraints (5.11)–(5.14).

With the assumed economic circumstances, there is enough information to compute equilibrium prices (5.23), consumption (5.18)–(5.21), and utility (5.16) at various points on the PPF (5.9). In particular, consider the outcomes where the quantity Q_1 of the first good (coconuts) takes one of the fifteen values 2, 4, ..., 14, 16, 17,..., 22, 23.[6] Table 5.4 shows utility values for both people, at each of these 15 points on the PPF, with person a being Crusoe and person b being Friday.

Utility values in Table 5.4 are higher toward the middle rows, with the middle-most row ($Q_1 = 16 = Q_2$) being the case of Crusoe monopoly in coconuts and Friday monopoly in fish. Perfect monopoly is Pareto efficient relative to all other rows in the table since in no other row are utility values at least as high for both people—and strictly higher for at least one person.[7] By the same criterion, there are five other Pareto efficient outcomes altogether, at $Q_1 = 12, 14, 16, 17, 18$. These include the cases where either Crusoe reduces hours in coconuts from eight to either six or seven, or Friday reduces hours in fish from either six or seven.

In Example 5.4.2, consumer happiness is no worse with total monopoly than with partial monopoly, both being Pareto efficient. The Pareto efficiency of total monopoly is valid in other cases too. For example, if Crusoe and Friday each work 12 hours a day, rather than 16, then

Table 5.4 Utility of consumption

Q1	Q2	Crusoe's utility	Friday's utility
2	23	4.4	2.4
4	22	6.0	3.4
6	21	6.9	4.3
8	20	7.6	5.1
10	19	8.0	5.8
12	18	8.2	6.5
14	17	8.2	7.3
16	16	8.0	8.0
17	14	7.3	8.2
18	12	6.5	8.2
19	10	5.8	8.0
20	8	5.1	7.6
21	6	4.3	6.9
22	4	3.4	6.0
23	2	2.4	4.4

there are nine Pareto efficient outcomes, each on the PPF, one of which is total monopoly. Or, if in Example 5.4.2 the preference for good 1 is now 0.25 and that of good 2 is 0.75, then there are seven Pareto efficient outcomes, one being total monopoly, the rest involving Friday as monopolist in fish and Crusoe as both fisherman and coconut gatherer. Also, if in Example 5.4.2 Crusoe's marginal products are now 20 coconut per hour and one fish per hour, there are two Pareto efficient outcomes, one total monopoly, the other having Friday as monopolist and Crusoe spending seven hours on coconuts and one hour on fish.

Monopoly, in one or more industries, is Pareto efficient among the opportunities provided by coordination production and exchange at equilibrium prices. But coordinated production need not provide as much consumer happiness to each person as the autarky situation where each person produces and consumes their own goods.

Example 5.4.3 In the Crusoe-Friday economy, let the situation be as in Example 5.4.2 but now suppose that Friday is much better than Crusoe is at gathering coconuts and fishing, having both an absolute advantage in each activity, as shown in Table 5.5 below.

Table 5.5 Marginal products, with production superstar Friday

Person	Coconuts	Fish
Crusoe	2	1
Friday	20	20

If Friday keeps to herself, producing and consuming only her own coconuts and fish, she will get the highest utility from putting four hours in coconut production, four hours in fishing, and getting $20 \times 4 = 80$ each of coconuts and fish, with utility equal to 80. On the other hand, if she coordinates production with the much less productive Crusoe, Crusoe specializing in coconuts and Friday in fish, in equilibrium with utility maximization Friday gets eight coconuts and 80 fish, losing out on 72 coconuts compared to autarky, and her utility is about 25.[8]

In Example 5.4.3 monopoly is good, in different senses and contexts: monopoly is good in autarky because it is Pareto efficient relative to opportunities available with coordinated production and exchange, and monopoly is good in the coordinated production context because it achieves productive efficiency and also Pareto efficiency relative to other exchange outcomes and autarky too.

If nobody in the two-person economy has a comparative advantage in producing a good, efficient coordinated production doesn't imply any monopoly—as discussed in Sect. 5.3. Moreover, a monopoly in each industry can make each person worse off utility-wise than some situation with no monopoly.

Example 5.4.4 In the Crusoe-Friday economy, let the situation be as in Example 5.4.2 but suppose now that Crusoe can collect one coconut or one fish, while Friday can collect two coconuts or two fish, as in Table 5.6 below.

Neither Crusoe nor Friday has a comparative advantage in coconuts or fish. If Crusoe specializes in coconuts and Friday specializes in fish, they together produce eight coconuts and 16 fish, each consuming four coconuts and eight fish in utility-maximizing equilibrium, , with utility $\sqrt{8 \times 4}$ or about 5.7. If instead Crusoe specializes in fish and Friday specializes in coconuts than both people consume eight coconuts and four

Table 5.6 Labor productivity, same for each person

Person	Coconuts	Fish
Crusoe	1	1
Friday	2	2

fish in equilibrium, with utility again about 5.7. On the other hand, if each person spends half their time in coconuts, half in fish, then together they produce 12 coconuts and 12 fish, and in equilibrium each consumes six coconuts and six fish, with utility $\sqrt{6 \times 6} = 6$. Here monopoly in each industry is worse than no monopoly, in terms of consumer happiness, though monopoly remains efficient in terms of production.

5.5   CONCLUSION

Monopoly is the situation where there is a single supplier of some good to society. The standing of monopoly, in relation to society, can be benign if having a single supplier is better—or no worse—than having more than one supplier. In a highly simplified version of the world, with only two people and two goods, monopoly can be benign, achieving productive efficiency, fairness of goods distribution, and consumer happiness or Pareto efficiency.

This chapter explores the desirability of monopoly. Monopoly is per force anti-competitive since its existence guarantees the nonexistence of competitors, and in that sense this chapter is also about anti-competitive behavior. The basic idea in this chapter applies more generally, but less precisely, to situations where there is a limited number suppliers to an industry, provided that those suppliers carry some comparative advantage in terms of productivity. On the other hand, the idea does not apply to purely opportunistic forms of anti-competitive behavior, such as price-fixing among firms in an industry, because they involve no production efficiency gains.

Some readers may find suspect the idea that monopoly may be good, especially if that argument involves some complicated-looking calculations or technical work—under the banner of a simple economic model. The idea that comparative advantage can make monopoly good is a restatement of the idea that countries can benefit if they specialize in particular industries and then trade specific goods with each other. Critics of international trade, and its comparative advantage rationale, will have plenty to criticize in the idea that comparative advantage can rationalize monopoly.

The fundamental complexity in this chapter arises not from mathematical modeling but from the simultaneous consideration of two industries at once. With two industries, efficient coordination of production factors is inherently complex. Adding to that trade and consumer satisfaction or happiness makes the economist's mental balancing act more arduous, the gateway to the foreboding realm of general equilibrium analysis. This book does not attempt about general equilibrium analysis on a grand scale, but it does carry on the balancing act of considering two or more industries at once. Such considerations become necessary when talking in depth about anti-competitive behavior linked to vertical integration or merging of firms, for example, or consumer effects of price-fixing in a parts industry that supplies to a consumer product manufacturer.

The overarching theme of this book is that monopoly and other forms of anti-competitive behavior are sometimes bad and can cause economic damages. This first chapter has characterized a good sort of monopoly, and the remaining chapters in Part 1 of the book continue this effort. Part 2 presents bad monopolies as the antithesis of good ones, lacking those virtuous characteristics that make good monopolies good. For relevant background on the economics of international trade see Ethier (1983), Krugman and Obstfeld (2009), and Van den Berg (2012).

5.6   PROBLEMS

1. Three virtuous properties for an economy to have are: (a) efficiency in production, (b) fairness in the distribution of goods to households, and (c) consumer happiness. Do you feel that the US economy generally achieves these virtues, and do you think that monopolies pose a threat to achieving them? Explain.

2. When goods are distributed to households, one way in which the distribution can be fair is if it distributes goods in proportion to the factors of production contributed by specific households, with more goods going to households that contribute more to production. An implication of this idea is that a person who own lots of land—and rents it out to big manufacturers—should get lots of money and so goods in return, even if that person inherited the land from their rich

parents. Does this arrangement sound fair in terms that make sense to you? Explain, and compare your reasoning here to your views about real-world monopoly.

3. The amount of goods that households consume is an important part of their living standards. High levels of consumption are generally desirable. A Pareto efficient pattern of household consumption is one in which no one consumer can be made better off without making others worse off. A monopoly can be Pareto efficient, but so can many other outcomes. Consider the situation where a benevolent dictator— or "social planner"—makes all people consume the same amount of goods. Explain why this is a Pareto efficient outcome for society, for a given amount of goods produced. Do you think it's better or worse than having markets for goods but also a monopoly in each industry?

4. In a two-person, two-good economy, if the two people coordinate their production efforts, then they will each tend to specialize in making one of the goods. Specialization can produce monopoly in each industry. Is monopoly of this sort consistent with the fact that people are coordinating their efforts? Explain.

5. In a two-person two-good economy with coordinated production and exchange at utility-maximizing equilibrium prices, if consumption utility is of the Cobb-Douglas type with each person having the same rates of preference—1/2 and 1/2 for goods 1 and 2—then in equilibrium each person has the same income, consumes the same amount of good 1, consumes the same amount of good 2, and enjoys the same amount of utility. This is true even if one person has much higher productivity in each industry. The equilibrium outcome is fair in the sense of Pareto efficiency. Does it seem fair to you more generally, given that one person may be much more productive than the other? Explain.

6. Crusoe and Friday are the only two people in a two-person, two-good economy. For each hour of labor, Crusoe can collect two coconuts or one fish. For each hour of labor Friday can collect two coconuts or two fish. Suppose that Crusoe and Friday have consumption preferences of the Cobb-Douglas type, with preference rate $w = 1/2$ for coconuts and rate $1 - w = 1/2$ for fish. Let the price of coconuts be $p_1 = 1$.

   (a) Who has an absolute advantage in coconuts? An absolute advantage in fish?

   (b) Who has a comparative advantage in coconuts? In fish?

   (c) Draw the production possibilities frontier (PPF), assuming that Crusoe and Friday coordinate their production efforts, using

Eq. (5.8) in the text. Label as point A on this curve the situation where each industry is a monopoly. How many coconuts and fish are produced at point A?

(d) At point A on your PPF from part c, who is the coconut monopolist? Who is the fish monopolist?

7. Continuing with the two-person two-good economy from Problem 5.6, answer the following, assuming that Crusoe and Friday coordinate their production plans, then exchange goods at equilibrium prices, with Crusoe a monopolist in coconuts and Friday a monopolist in fish.

(a) Find the equilibrium price p_2 of fish, using Eq. (5.23).

(b) Find the income levels Y for Crusoe and Friday, using prices and quantities of goods produced by each person.

(c) Find the consumption levels C for Crusoe and Friday, using Eqs. (5.18)–(5.21).

(d) Find utility of consumption U for Crusoe and Friday, using Eq. (5.16).

(e) Find utility of consumption U for Crusoe and Friday in the case of autarky where there is no coordinated production, Crusoe producing eight coconuts and four fish for himself, Friday producing eight coconuts and eight fish for herself. Compare autarky utility to the utility in part Which provides greater consumer happiness, monopoly autarky style or monopoly coordination style?

8. Crusoe and Friday are the only two people in a two-person, two-good economy, with each person working eight hours per day. For each hour of labor, Crusoe can collect one coconut or one fish, while Friday can collect two coconuts or two fish.[9]

(a) Who, if anyone, has an absolute advantage in producing coconuts? In producing fish?

(b) Draw the production possibilities frontier (PPF) for coordinated production, similar to Fig. 5.2 in the text, assuming that Crusoe and Friday coordinate their production efforts, using Eq. (5.8) in the text. Mark on the PPF the point at coordinates $(8, 16)$ and label it point A, mark the point at $(16, 8)$ and label it as point B, and mark the point $(12, 12)$ and label it as C.

(c) Show that points A on the PPF is achieved with Crusoe as monopolist in coconuts and Friday as monopolist in fish. Likewise, show that points B on the PPF is achieved with Crusoe as monopolist in fish and Friday as monopolist in coconuts. Show that point C

is achieved by Crusoe and Friday each spending half their time producing coconuts, the other half producing fish.

(d) Show that points A and B can occur as non-monopoly outcomes, as follows. Show that point A is achieved with Friday working full time in coconut collection and Crusoe working half-time in coconuts, half-time in fish. Show that point B is achieved with Crusoe working full time in coconut collection and Friday working half-time in coconuts, half-time in fish.

(e) If Crusoe and Friday each like coconuts and fish the same, which of points A, B, C seems the most desirable outcome? As a check, suppose that Crusoe and Friday exchange goods at equilibrium prices, and that each has Cobb-Douglas preferences for consumption, with rate of preference $1/2$ for coconuts and for fish. Find incomes, equilibrium prices, and consumption amounts. Using these, show the following:

   (i) Utility for Crusoe and Friday equals $\sqrt{4 \times 8}$ at points A and B, and equals 6 at point C.

   (ii) A monopoly in each industry leads to lower utility for each person than the situation where each person splits half their time working in each industry.

9. In a two-person two-good economy with coordinated production and exchange of goods at equilibrium prices, monopoly in each industry can be a good economic outcome. Exchange, at equilibrium prices, is not necessarily an arrangement that would develop in a world with only two people. Suppose instead that the two people coordinate in production, each becoming a monopolist in one industry, and that the two people then fail to agree on any trade deal, each consuming only what he or she has produced. Assume that each person has Cobb-Douglas consumption preferences, with preference rate $w = 1/2$ for the first good and rate $1 - w = 1/2$ for the second good.

   (a) Show that the failure to trade causes each person to have utility U equal to 0.

   (b) If, instead of coordinating production, each person is in autarky and producing one unit of each good, show that utility u equals one for each person.

   (c) Given that autarky is better than specialization and no trade, suggest a way that the two people might reach a reasonable trade deal and improve an autarky in terms of production efficiency and consumer happiness, even if the economy never reaches competitive equilibrium.

Table 5.7   Labor productivity

Person	Coconuts	Fish
Crusoe	2	1
Friday	1	2

10. In an economy with two people (Crusoe and Friday) and two goods (coconuts and fish), suppose that each person works two hours per day, with goods produced per hour shown in Table 5.7.

    Assume that each person has Cobb-Douglas utility preferences, and that the rate of preference for each good is the same. Also, assume that Crusoe and Friday coordinate production and exchange goods at equilibrium prices. Create a table analogous to Table 5.4 in the text, showing utility values at points on the production possibility frontier, assuming that Crusoe spends either one or two hours producing coconuts, and Friday spends either one or two hours producing fish. Your table should have three rows of numbers. Which rows in the table represent Pareto efficient outcomes? Does monopoly in each industry provide consumer happiness? Explain.

11. Repeat Problem the rates of preference equal to 0.25 for the first good and 0.75 for the second good. Does the conclusion about monopoly change with this change in technical assumptions?

12. Repeat Problem Crusoe producing 20 coconuts per hour instead of two. Does the conclusion about monopoly change with this change in technical assumptions?

NOTES

1. The story is adapted from the classic tale by Daniel Defoe, in a couple of variants, the first one in which Crusoe is alone, the second in which he has a companion—as in the book.
2. Via formulas (5.7) and (5.10)
3. If, in addition, Friday really likes fish but doesn't much like coconuts then neither person may be willing to specialize and exchange deal with the other.
4. If Friday works four hours in coconuts and four hours in fish, from Table 5.2 she gets $4 \times 10 = 40$ coconuts and $4 \times 20 = 80$ fish.
5. Assume that coconuts and fish are perishable, lasting only a day.
6. The first seven values $2, 4, \ldots, 14$ are where Friday specializes in fish, but Crusoe works at both coconuts at fish. The last seven values $16, 17, \ldots, 22$

are where Crusoe specializes in coconuts, but Friday works at both coconuts and fish. The middle or eighth value, 16, is where both Crusoe specializes in coconuts and Friday specializes in fish.

7. This equilibrium outcome is Pareto efficient among the trades that Crusoe and Friday could have made from their totally specialized endowments, an instance of what economists call the First Fundamental Welfare Theorem of economics.

8. With Cobb-Douglas utility and first good preference $w = 1/2$, Friday's utility of consumption in the autarky situation is $8^w(80)^{1-w} = 8(1/2)(80)^{1/2}$, which is about 25.

9. This is the same as Example 5.4.3 and Table 5.6 in the text, and this problem invites the reader to work on Example 5.4.3 in more detail.

References

Ethier, W. (1983). *Modern international economics.* New York, NY: W.W. Norton Co.

Krugman, P. R., & Obstfeld, M. (2009). *International economics: Theory and policy* (8th ed.). Boston, MA: Pearson Addison Wesley.

Van den Berg, H. (2012). *International economics: A heterodox approach* (2nd ed.) Armonk, NY: M.E. Sharpe.

CHAPTER 6

Natural Monopoly

Abstract Antitrust economics deals with situations of high market concentration and anti-competitive harm in a given industry, with a focus on the activities of private companies. One of the government's tools to deal with antitrust issues is industry regulation, via the Federal Trade Commission (FTC), the Federal Communications Commission (FCC), and similar agencies. Industry regulation applies to private companies but also to publicly owned or quasi-private companies, common examples being utilities—electric companies, water companies, and so on. Such companies are often referred to as "natural monopolies," the subject of this chapter.

Efficiencies of production scale can justify a monopoly—elevating it to the status of natural monopoly. This efficiency argument is not unlike those stated earlier about pure monopoly and international trade. This chapter covers some simple models of scale economies, and their implications for market concentration. Constant returns to scale, an assumption implicit in earlier chapters of this book, differs from increasing returns to scale—a situation where natural monopoly is in consumers' interest.

As in Chap. 5 on international trade, the modeling framework here is general equilibrium—with a role for household labor and consumption choices. Increasing returns makes natural monopoly efficient and consumers happy, even without regulation of monopoly price, because all households are assumed to have equal access to production opportunities.

© The Author(s) 2018
S. Gilbert, *Multi-Market Antitrust Economics,* Quantitative
Perspectives on Behavioral Economics and Finance,
https://doi.org/10.1007/978-3-319-69386-6_6

Excluded from the model is access inequality or wealth concentration that could lead the monopoly to under-provide or overcharge the typical consumer, and so be deserving of price *regulation*. Wealth concentration is a well-known feature of the world's economic landscape, and like market concentration can lead to inefficiencies, unfairness, or inequality. A detailed study of price regulation exceeds the scope of this book, but the reader is invited to consider more generally how wealth concentration affects the fairness of the various market situations discussed in this book.

Monopoly, and more generally cases of high market concentration, can be good in a big economy. Chapter 5 discussed the sense in which monopoly can be good in a small economy—with two people and two goods. The main idea there was that comparative advantages in the productivity of different people can lead to efficient coordination of goods production, with labor specialization and monopoly in industries run by different people. This same idea applies, at least in principle, to an economy with many people and many goods, with each person producing only those goods in which they have a comparative advantage in productivity, relative some other people. Specialization leads to a relatively small number of firms, each staffed by people with relatively high productivity in the relevant industry. But unlike in the two-person two-good economy, a monopoly in one or more industries is not generally required for production efficiency, at least not in the sense of monopoly being a one-person firm. A study of monopoly in this setting is possible but complicated.

To discuss monopoly in the context of a large economy, from here on in this chapter will ignore differences in productivity between workers, focusing instead on how the total amount of work done relates to the amount of good produced in a given industry. The production function, in a given industry, shows the quantity of a good produced at each possible quantity of those factors of production used to produce the good. In this chapter, all factors aside from labor are assumed to be in fixed amount, and the production function relates the output-of-goods quantity to input-of-labor quantity.

Keywords Production • Returns to scale • Natural monopoly

6.1 PRODUCTION AND RETURNS TO SCALE

In a given industry, with a single input (labor), the scale of production is identified by the amount of input in use. Production scales up when more work is done. The return to scale, with a single input, is the ratio of additional output to additional input. If the return to scale is the same for any amount of input, then production is said to have constant returns to scale. If the return to scale falls when the input amount rises, then production has decreasing returns to scale, while if the return to scale rises when input rises, then production has increasing returns to scale.[1]

To illustrate constant returns to scale, consider lawn mowing. Each additional hour of mowing produces the same additional amount of lawn mowed, assuming that productivity remains the same during the mowing process. As a result, the ratio of lawn area mowed to mowing hours is likely about the same for short mows and long mows.

If a worker gradually tires during a work day, productivity near day's end may be less than at the beginning. More generally, if labor productivity tends to fall off when the number of labor hours done is higher, the ratio of output to input will tend to fall at higher input levels, creating decreasing returns to scale. Significantly decreasing returns to scale are common in many industries, especially in situations where firms try to boost production from normal amounts to exceptional amounts.

A relatively large scale of production is sometimes necessary to produce a good, leading to increasing returns to scale. While a person can mow a lawn alone, they likely cannot build a house alone. It may require 1000 work hours by a construction crew of 20 workers, to build one house of common size. Any less than 1000 hours produces no finished houses.

Returns to scale have important effects on the production efficiency of large-scale versus small-scale businesses. Decreasing returns to scale favor relatively small firms, increasing returns favor large firms. Constant returns favor neither large nor small firms.

A monopoly can be beneficial—or at least not harmful—in industries with constant or increasing returns to scale. In such industries, production efficiency can be achieved by putting all production under the roof of a single company—a monopoly. Sections 6.2 and 6.3 explore this idea in detail. Like Chap. 5, these sections also discuss the fairness of goods distribution to households, and consumer happiness or utility, in connection with monopoly.

6.2   CONSTANT RETURNS TO SCALE

Let the economy be populated by any number of people, and call this number n. It's sometimes useful to label a typical person as person i, where i is a number ranging from 1 to n: $i = 1, 2, \ldots, n$. In this economy with potentially many people, suppose there are two goods: good 1 and good 2, suppose further that each person is able to produce c_1 units of good 1 for each hour of labor spent on good one. Similarly, each person is able to produce c_2 units of good 2 for each hour of labor spent producing it. As in Chap. 5, let L stand for labor hours—up to $\bar{L}$ hours per day, and let Q stand for quantity of goods produced.

The production functions, linking L to Q for each person, have constant returns to scale, as stated in equation form below.

Individual Production Functions, Constant Returns to Scale

$$Q_{i1} = c_1 L_{i1}, i = 1, 2, \ldots, n \tag{6.1}$$

$$Q_{i2} = c_2 L_{i2}, i = 1, 2, \ldots, n \tag{6.2}$$

In Chap. 5 there were only two people producing goods, whereas now there is any number n of them, and this adds complexity but at the same time each person now has the same productivity in a given industry, whereas Chap. 5 allowed people to have different productivity rates within a given industry.

For each good, let production take place at a person's home—which is also a factory. There are n such factories, and each can accommodate up to n workers. In other words, each person can leave their home/factory and work at any other person's home/factory. Suppose each person produces a given good only at one factory. Let each factory in which good 1 is actually produced be identified as a firm, producing good 1, and similarly let each factory producing good 2 be a firm in that industry. There are then up to n firms in each industry. A monopoly exists in an industry if all of the good in that industry is made at a single factory.

To determine whether a monopoly in some industry might be good when there are constant returns to scale, let L_1 and L_2 be the total quantities of labor spent on goods 1 and 2, and let Q_1 and Q_2 be the total quantities of output produced. Applying the person-specific production

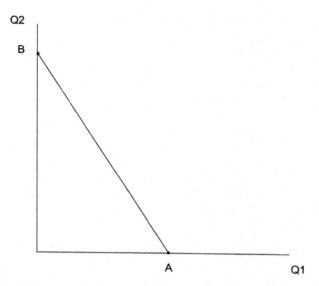

Fig. 6.1   Production possibility frontier, constant returns to scale

functions (6.1)–(6.2), the industry-wide production functions are of the same form:

Industry Production Functions, Constant Returns to Scale

$$Q_1 = c_1 L_1, i = 1, 2, \ldots, n \qquad (6.3)$$
$$Q_2 = c_2 L_2, i = 1, 2, \ldots, n \qquad (6.4)$$

The following graph shows the economy's production possibilities frontier (PPF) with constant returns to scale:

In Fig. 6.1, the point A represents the situation where only good 1 is produced, a total of $c_1 n \bar{L}$ units, while at B only good 2 is produced, a total of $c_2 n \bar{L}$ units.

Any point on society's PPF achieves production efficiency, and this includes every possible situation where each person works full-time, $\bar{L}$ hours per day, producing some good(s) at some factories. Among these possibilities is the case of monopoly in each industry, with just one factory for each good produced.

Monopoly achieves production efficiency, when there are constant returns to scale and no productivity differences between laborers, regardless of how many people are in the economy. In these terms, monopoly is good when there are constant returns to scale.

Other criteria by which monopoly can be judged good or bad are the fairness of goods distribution to households and the happiness of consumers. To apply these criteria, suppose that each person takes home the amount of goods they made, and that all people either consume their own goods or trade goods with other people at equilibrium prices, so as to maximize their utility of consumption. Also, suppose that each person has Cobb-Douglas utility preferences, with a common preference rate w for good 1, and rate $1 - w$ for good 2.

With each person taking home exactly what they produce, goods distribution is fair in terms discussed earlier, and this is true in the monopoly situation—where everyone works at one person's home/factor—as well as in other work arrangements. The assumption that people take home only what they produce appears to ignore the principle of trade or exchange benefits, but in the present case, each person will achieve the highest utility of consumption by producing goods 1 and 2 and consuming them directly. Any coordination with others, in production, does not generate any efficiencies or new opportunities for anyone. This is because each person has the same productivity for each hour worked, and each is assumed able to take home what they produce.

To further describe consumer choice and happiness, for typical individual i, let C_{i1} be their consumption of the first good, and let C_{2i} be their consumption of the second good. Consuming only what they produce, consumption choices are limited by the number of hours L_{i1} and L_{i2} that person i spends on goods 1 and 2, respectively. Total hours must add to $\bar{L}$, as in Eqs. (5.1)–(5.2) in Chap. 5, and given productivity levels c_1 and c_2 in the 2 industries, consumption choices are constrained as in the following equation:

$$\frac{C_{i1}}{m_1} + \frac{C_{i2}}{m_2} = \bar{L} \qquad (6.5)$$

The utility-maximizing choice of consumption amounts, subject to the consumption constraint (6.5), depends on labor productivity in the two industries and on consumer preference for the two goods, as shown in the following two equations.

$$C_{i1} = \bar{L}m_1 w,$$ (6.6)

$$C_{i2} = \bar{L}m_2(1 - w)$$ (6.7)

To achieve these consumption levels, individual i works $L_{i1} = \bar{L}w$ hours producing good 1, and $L_{i2} = \bar{L}(1 - w)$ hours producing good 2.

While trade is possible, each person's labor and consumption levels are the same with or without trade at equilibrium prices. In equilibrium, with good 1 the numeraire good, its price p is set to 1, as in Chap. 5, and the price of the second good is given by Eq. (5.23) in Chap. 5, which here simplifies to:

$$p_2^* = \frac{m_1}{m_2}$$ (6.8)

At equilibrium prices, person i has income $Y_i = \bar{L}m_1$ and their consumption levels are the same as in the no-trade outcome described by Eqs. (6.6) and (6.7).

With or without trade, each person consumes the same amount of goods, and enjoys the same amount of utility.[2] This is true if each person works at the same factory—the monopoly case—or if they don't. Consumer happiness, with utility-maximizing labor and consumption choices, is the same with monopoly as without it, and monopoly is Pareto efficient.

With constant returns to scale, monopoly achieves the same levels of production efficiency and Pareto efficiency as do situations with any number of firms in a given industry.[3] Also, monopoly is fair, in terms of goods distribution, assuming that people can take home their own product. Monopoly is good, or at least not bad, in these terms.

Example 6.2.1 There are ten people in an economy with two goods, returns to scale being constant and given by $m_1 = 1$ in industry 1, $m_2 = 3$ in industry 2. Each person works the same number $\bar{L} = 8$ of hours per day, and has the same Cobb-Douglas consumption preferences—with rate of preference $w_1 = 3/4$ for the first good.

If people make choices so as to maximize the utility of consumption then, applying Eqs. (6.6) and (6.7), they each produce and consume $\bar{L}m_1w = 8(1)(3/4) = 6$ units of good 1 and $\bar{L}m_2(1 - w) = 8(3)(1/4) = 6$ units of good 2. The total amount of goods produced is 60 in each industry, with six contributed by each of ten people. With the opportunity to exchange goods, equilibrium prices are $p_1^* = 1$ and, applying Eq. (6.8), $p_2^* = m_1/m_2 = 1/3$. However, no trade occurs in equilibrium, and people retain their endowments of goods. The economic outcome achieves production efficiency, goods distribution fairness, and consumer happiness, and can occur with each industry organized as a monopoly or instead with up to ten firms per industry.

6.3   INCREASING RETURNS TO SCALE

Suppose that there are constant returns to scale in the first industry but increasing returns in the second. For the first good, the ratio Q/L of quantity to labor remains the same at each amount of labor, but for the second good this ratio rises as L gets bigger, as shown in Fig. 6.2.

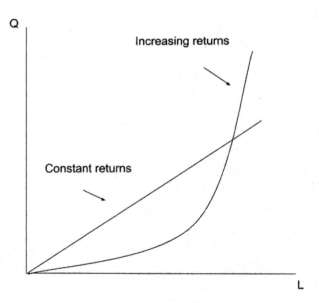

Fig. 6.2   Production functions, constant and increasing returns

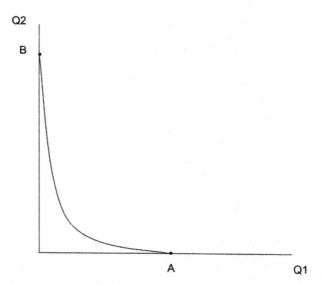

Fig. 6.3 PPF, increasing returns in second industry

With just two goods in the economy, the first having constant returns and the second having increasing returns, the production possibilities frontier has a bowed downward or convex shape, as shown in Fig. 6.3.
At point A in Fig. 6.3, everyone spends all their time making the first good, while at point B they spend all their time making the second.

Let each person's labor productivity in the first industry be as described earlier in the constant returns to scale situation. With marginal product m_1, the ith worker puts L_{1i} units of labor in to product 1 and takes home $m_1 L_{1i}$ units of product. For the second industry, with increasing returns to scale, each person's marginal product for the second good is increasing in the amount of their own labor and the labor of others. Laborers' individual contributions to total output depend on what other laborers are contributing, a different situation than having each worker make and take home their own product.

In industry 2, suppose as earlier people can work at any of $i = 1, 2, \ldots, n$ factories. For any one of these factories, let Q_{2k} be the amount of goods produced by that factory, where $k = 1, 2, \ldots, n$. For any given factory k, let output depend on labor as input as follows:

$$Q_{2k} = f_2(L_{2k}), k = 1, 2, \ldots, n \tag{6.9}$$

with notation f_2 representing the production function—linking input to output.[4] With increasing returns to scale in the second industry, the production function $f_2(L_{2k})$ becomes steeper as L_{2k} gets bigger, at each factory k. The total output Q_2 is the sum of outputs Q_{2k} across factories, and likewise total labor L_2 is the sum of factory-specific labor L_{2k}. At each factory, the total amount of labor L_{2k} is the sum of individual labor hours L_{i2k} for individuals $i = 1, 2, \ldots, n$, and since only the total hours matter, workers are indistinguishable except in the amount of work they do. Suppose that worker i receives a share $Q_{2k}(L_{k2i}/L_{k2})$ of the second good in proportion to their labor contribution to each factory k they work at in the second industry.

On the production possibilities frontier (PPF), with increasing returns to scale in industry 2, everyone works at the same factory in that industry, nobody works at the others. With factory synonymous for firm, there is a monopoly in good 2. In good 1, with constant returns to scale, on the PPF there may be monopoly or not, each providing the same output. Monopoly is beneficial in industry 2, providing superior production efficiency over non-monopoly patterns of industrial organization. Monopoly is also possibly beneficial—and at least harmless—in industry 1.

To check out consumer happiness in the context of monopoly and increasing returns to scale in an industry, let the production function for good 2 take the form:

$$Q_2 = dL_2^e \tag{6.10}$$

for some positive numbers d and g and each amount of labor L_2. With increasing returns to scale, the function $f_2(L_2) = eL_2^e$ is convex, in which case the exponent g must be greater than 1.

With each person i having the same consumption preferences and also the same role in production, they can achieve the greatest consumption happiness by putting the same number of hours L_{i1} into the first industry, and likewise the same number of hours into the second industry, in which case $L_{i1} = L_1/n$ and $L_{i2} = L_2/n$. Consumption levels are:

$$C_{i1} = \frac{m_1}{n}L_1 \tag{6.11}$$

$$C_{2i} = \frac{d}{n}L_2^g \tag{6.12}$$

To maximize consumer happiness, suppose each person has the same Cobb-Douglas type utility function, as earlier. The best consumption choice is the one that maximizes utility subject to the overall resource constraint on the n laborers:

$$L_1 + L_2 = n\bar{L} \tag{6.13}$$

Utility maximization requires that the tradeoff or marginal rate of substitution (MRS), between consuming-producing labor amounts L_1 and L_2, be equal to the marginal rate of transformation (MRT) of switching work hours in one industry to those in another.

Equating MRS with MRT imposes the following restriction on L_1 and L_2:

$$L_2 = \left(\frac{1 - w}{w}\frac{m_1}{d}L_1\right)^{1/g} \tag{6.14}$$

The unique solution to Eqs. (6.13) and (6.14) provides the optimal values of L_1 and L_2, together with the optimal consumption levels via Eqs. (6.11) and (6.12).

Consumer happiness is greatest with a monopoly in industry 2 and does not require trade in either industry. If exchange is made available, then, in equilibrium, each person keeps their endowment or income and the consumption levels they prefer in the absence of exchange.

Example 6.3.1 There are ten people in an economy with two goods, returns to scale being constant in industry 1 and increasing in industry 2. The industry production functions are $Q_1 = L1$ and $Q_2 = (1/100)L^3$. Each person works eight hours a day and has Cobb-Douglas utility of consumption with preference rate $w = 1/2$ for good 1.

Applying Eqs. (6.13) and (6.14), and searching among candidate values of L_1 that make these equations true—or nearly so—results in values

$L_1 = 44.55$ and $L_2 = 35.45$. Applying consumption equations (6.11) and (6.12), consumption, per person is $C_{i1} = (m_1/n)L_1 = (1/10)(44.55) = 4.455$ and $C_{i2} = (d/n)L_2^g = ((1/1000)/10)(35.45)^3 = 445.5$.

With optimal production and consumption choices, industry 2 is a monopoly and industry 1 may be a monopoly—or not. Total production is $Q_1 = 44.55$ in industry 1 and $Q_2 = 4455$ in industry 2. With exchange at equilibrium prices, prices are $p_1^* = 1$ and $p_2^* = ((1 - w)/w)Q_1/Q_2 = 44.55/4455 = 0.01$.

6.4   NATURAL MONOPOLY

Increasing returns to scale create a natural monopoly, one which is efficient production-wise, more so than situations with more than one supplier. Natural monopoly is desirable provided that it is paired with a mechanism for fair distribution of goods to households. If, as in the increasing returns to scale model discussed earlier, each worker plays the same role in producing the good, a fair distribution can be based on hours put into production.

A public utility, such as provider of water to a town, is a practical example of increasing returns to scale. Such utilities are often described as natural monopolies. If such a utility is privately owned by an individual or a group other than the firm's workers, there is no guarantee that workers will be compensated in proportion to the value they add to the production process. Too, with utilities being necessities there is the risk that the firm providing them will charge a very high price—not the Walrasian equilibrium price discussed earlier. The real world has institutions, including regulatory agencies, that tend to make public utilities act in the interest of the typical household.

To regulate a utility, the government can consider a price ceiling, forcing the utility to charge consumers a price less than the monopolist's preferred price—where marginal revenue equals marginal cost. If a price ceiling can be determined that eliminates unwarranted or excess profit, but keeps the utility's owners willing to continue the business, then the result may be socially optimal. In the model discussed earlier, natural monopoly had no "excess" profits because all households had equal access to firms' production opportunities.[5]

Earlier, in Chap. 2, a pure monopoly could earn excess profits by cutting production back to a level less than what competitive equilibrium would provide, setting marginal cost equal to marginal revenue, not equal to price. Competitive equilibrium is the benchmark or reference point for measuring the pure monopolist's excess profits. If there are increasing returns to scale, competitive equilibrium—with many firms—may not be a sensible benchmark for measuring monopoly profits. Ideally, price controls on regulated natural monopolies maintain an incentive for the monopolies to keep operating while cutting price to a degree that reflects society's sense of fairness and efficiency.

6.5 CONCLUSION

Monopolies are often big companies, behemoths. Such behemoths make sense in terms of production efficiency if it's hard to provide a good or service reliably without massive scale. Monopoly can also make sense when a grand scale is not needed but is no less efficient than a small scale. This chapter stated these production ideas more systematically, via returns to scale. The situation where industry scale does not affect efficiency is called constant returns to scale, and in that context monopoly is good, or at least not bad, and is compatible with the idea of monopoly with a competitive fringe. The situation where industry scale positively effects efficiency is called increasing returns to scale, and in that context monopoly is clearly good and also compatible with the idea of natural monopoly.

This chapter identifies situations where monopoly can be good, or at least not bad. These situations are highly simplified versions of what might be going on in a particular industry, and they take the form of economic models. In the present chapter, the models are more realistic than in Chap. 5 in that sense that they can accommodate many people and also a return to scale that varies with the scale of production. On the other hand, these models assume that workers are all the same, in terms of productivity, whereas in Chap. 5 workers are allowed to have productivity advantages over one another. To achieve more realism in some aspects of the economic model, while limiting the overall complexity of the model, some realism is sacrificed in other aspects of the model.

The reader should not be guiled into thinking that the economic models in this chapter, or elsewhere in this book, are necessarily useful for any purpose other than assaying the benefits and costs of monopoly and related phenomena. Economic models are developed by economists, and it's safe to assume that your typical economist cannot manufacture a car, build a telecommunications network, or produce much of anything besides economic research, instruction, presentation, consultation, and debate. The economist's idea of production function is highly simplified, and could not be relied on to produce any real good or service. Yet the idea of productivity, linking inputs to outputs, is simple and important when thinking about industry scale and monopoly. Economic models, that showcase productivity, allow for a systematic exploration of how productivity patterns can affect choices and industrial organization.

6.6   PROBLEMS

1. Explain how the production idea of constant returns to scale relates to the desirability of monopoly in an industry.
2. Explain how the production idea of increasing returns to scale relates to the desirability of monopoly in an industry.
3. Explain how constant returns to scale in an industry can give rise to a monopoly with a competitive fringe.
4. In an industry that produces a good using a single input—labor— production has decreasing returns to scale if the ratio of goods output quantity to labor input quantity falls, as the amount of labor used by a firm increases. In terms of production efficiency, is a monopoly likely to be efficient in an industry with decreasing returns to scale? Explain.
5. For an industry, monopoly is most clearly advantageous in which situation: constant returns to scale, or increasing returns to scale? Explain.
6. Suppose it takes six hours to mow an acre's worth of lawn in a residential neighborhood.
   (a) What is the return to scale in the lawn mowing industry?
   (b) Is this industry a likely candidate for monopoly? Why or why not?
7. In the homebuilding industry, pouring concrete, raising walls, and laying roofing shingles are all situations where workers are more productive in a team than by themselves. Relate these situations to the idea of increasing returns to scale.
8. Cirque Du Soleil is a company that puts on shows performed by a troupe of diverse actors, acrobats, stunt performers, and musicians. You may have seen one of their shows in person. If not, go online a look at a promotional clip or review of one of their shows. In what sense does a Cirque Du Soleil show involve increasing returns to scale?

9. Explain how an industry with increasing returns to scale can give rise to a natural monopoly.
10. Which of the following most strikingly exhibits increasing returns to scale, and would be most likely to become a natural monopoly: a frozen yogurt shop, or a railroad that provides railroad service nationwide? Explain.
11. What is the difference between a natural monopoly and a monopoly with a competitive fringe?
12. In an economy with two goods and ten people, suppose that each industry has constant returns to scale, and let the return to scale be $m_1 = 1$ in industry 1 and $m_2 = 2$ in industry 2. Suppose also that each person has Cobb-Douglas type utility of consumption, with preference rate $w = 1/2$ for good 1.
    (a) How many hours will each person work in industry 1? In industry 2?
    (b) How much will each person consume of good 1? Good 2?
    (c) With goods exchange at equilibrium prices, what is the price of the second good?
    (d) In what sense is a monopoly good, or not bad, in this economy?
13. In an economy with two goods and ten people, suppose that each industry has constant returns to scale, and let the return to scale be $m_1 = 1$ in industry 1 and $m_2 = 1$ in industry 2. Suppose also that each person has Cobb-Douglas type utility of consumption, with preference rate $w = 1/4$ for good 1.
    (a) How many hours will each person work in industry 1? In industry 2?
    (b) How much will each person consume of good 1? Good 2?
    (c) With goods exchange at equilibrium prices, what is the price of the second good?
    (d) In what sense is a monopoly good, or not bad, in this economy?
14. In an economy with two goods and three people, suppose that the first industry has constant returns to scale and that the second industry has increasing returns to scale. Suppose the return to scale in the first industry is $m_1 = 1$ and that output quantity in the second industry is $Q_2 = L_2^2$, with L_2 the amount of labor in that industry. Also, suppose that each person has Cobb-Douglas utility preferences, with preference rate $w = 1/2$ for the first good.
    (a) On a single graph, plot the production functions for the two industries.

(b) Find the return to scale in the second industry with one unit of labor and also with ten units of labor. Is the return to scale higher with more labor?

(c) Is monopoly in each industry efficient, from a production stand-point?

15. Suppose that the economy is as described in Problem 6.6.

(a) How many hours will each person work in industry 1? In industry 2?

(b) How much will each person consume of good 1? Good 2?

(c) With goods exchange at equilibrium prices, what is the price of the second good?

(c) In what sense is a monopoly good, or not bad, in this economy?

16. Do Problems 6.6 and 6.6, and then redo them under the assumption that the preference rate for the first good is $w = 3/4$ rather than $w = 1/4$. How do the optimal amounts of consumption and production change? Assuming that optimal choices are made, is there a monopoly in the second industry?

17. Do Problems 6.6 and 6.6, and then redo them under the assumption that, in the second industry, any one factory can hold at most two of the three workers. What is the most efficient production plan now? How do the optimal amounts of consumption and production change? What is the utility value of each person? Are consumers as happy with this situation as they are in the monopoly outcome of Problem 6.6?

NOTES

1. Returns to scale are important for explaining differences in firm size across industries and are an essential element of classical economic theory, see, for example, Hirshleifer (1984), Kreps (1990), Mas-Colell et al. (1995), Nicholson and Snyder (2012), and Varian (1992).

2. With the assumed Cobb-Douglas form of utility function, each person's utility of consumption—with optimally chosen work and consumption levels—is $U = (wm_1)^w((1 - w)m_2)^{1-w}\bar{L}$.

3. With n people, each having a house/factory, the maximum number of firms is n.

4. Industry 1 also has a production function: $Q_1 = f_1(L_1)$, of the straight-line or linear form $f_1(L_1) = m_1 L_1$. For any given factory k producing good 1, its output is $Q_{1k} = f_1(L_{1k})$, with L_{1k} the amount of work done at that factory.

5. For more on the regulation of monopoly see Harrison et al. (2004) and Decker (2014).

REFERENCES

Decker, C. (2014). *Modern economic regulation: An introduction to theory and practice.* New York, NY: Cambridge University Press.

Harrison, J. L., Morgan, T. D., & Verkuil, P. R. (2004). *Regulation and deregulation: Cases and materials* (2nd ed.). New York, NY: West Academic Publishing.

Hirshleifer, J. (1984). *Price theory and applications* (3rd ed.). Englewood Cliffs, NJ: Prentice-Hall.

Kreps, D. M. (1990). *A course in microeconomic theory.* Princeton, NJ: Princeton University Press.

Mas-Colell, A., Whinston, M. D., & Green, J. R. (1995). *Microeconomic theory.* New York, NY: Oxford University Press.

Nicholson, W., & Snyder, C. (2012). *Microeconomic theory: Basic principles and extenstions* (12th ed.). Boston, MA: Cengage Learning.

Varian, H. R. (1992). *Microeconomic analysis* (3rd ed.). New York, NY: W.W. Norton and Company.

INDEX

Note: Page numbers followed by "n" refers to notes.

© The Author(s) 2018

S. Gilbert, *Multi-Market Antitrust Economics*, Quantitative Perspectives on Behavioral Economics and Finance, https://doi.org/10.1007/978-3-319-69386-6

132   INDEX

Printed by Printforce, United Kingdom